A YOUNG LIFE IN YOUR HANDS

A YOUNG LIFE IN YOUR HANDS

James Lahiff

A YOUNG LIFE IN YOUR HANDS

Copyright © 2022 James Lahiff.

All rights reserved. No part of this book may be used or reproduced by any means, graphic, electronic, or mechanical, including photocopying, recording, taping or by any information storage retrieval system without the written permission of the author except in the case of brief quotations embodied in critical articles and reviews.

iUniverse books may be ordered through booksellers or by contacting:

iUniverse
1663 Liberty Drive
Bloomington, IN 47403
www.iuniverse.com
844-349-9409

Because of the dynamic nature of the Internet, any web addresses or links contained in this book may have changed since publication and may no longer be valid. The views expressed in this work are solely those of the author and do not necessarily reflect the views of the publisher, and the publisher hereby disclaims any responsibility for them.

Any people depicted in stock imagery provided by Getty Images are models, and such images are being used for illustrative purposes only.
Certain stock imagery © Getty Images.

ISBN: 978-1-6632-3891-7 (sc)
ISBN: 978-1-6632-3890-0 (e)

Library of Congress Control Number: 2022907695

Print information available on the last page.

iUniverse rev. date: 05/26/2022

For Ruth, Jannette, Patrick,
Ralph, Jenny, Julie, and Jack

Contents

Preface ix

In the Town Where It Happened 1
Here Comes the Sun 6
It's a Blue World 14
Praise the Lord and Pass the Ammunition 19
Beginning to See the Light 33
There'll Be Some Changes Made 44
Don't Stop Thinking About Tomorrow 57
Sum Sum Summertime 72
At the (S)hop 88
Biding My Time 96
Heigh-Ho, Heigh-Ho 105
See You Later, Alligator 118

Preface

It was mid-February, early in the evening, and I was in my usual spot on the sofa, at home in Athens, Georgia. Lying flat on my back and semiconscious, I was dividing my attention between the network news on the television and a newspaper. I came to life when I heard my hometown, Marinette, Wisconsin, mentioned. A local man, who had been a key figure in an international military incident, was being interviewed. The incident, known as the Iran-Contra Affair, had occurred a decade or so earlier, and the interview was intended to update the viewers on what the man had done since then. It turns out that he was simply enjoying life back in his hometown, not very gripping stuff for a national audience.

At the conclusion of the interview, however, when the suave anchor from New York City asked the equally polished reporter what it was like "up there," the reporter was far from complimentary. He unloaded. He thought that the place was unbelievable, located in the middle of nowhere and not even close to anything of interest. While some of the local citizens had been saying that same thing for years, that was tolerable because every community has a certain percentage of misguided souls. Hearing it on the national news was quite different and unsettling. It was irritating to know that the reporter had been in the community for a single day, even more so to think of the nationwide audience that was exposed to the falsehoods.

It stung to realize the effect this blasphemy would have on the vast number of Americans who had undoubtedly intended to visit this community. They would now delete that planned trip from their bucket list. This was my hometown that was being disparaged, the center of my universe during my formative years. It was here that my value system formed, dreams were dreamed, goals were set, and a few of those goals were almost accomplished. Then and there, I vowed to write my story and to eliminate any negative perceptions that may still linger about living "up there."

Being somewhat of a procrastinator, it has taken me several decades to get started, but the time has come. My account is based on my memories, refreshed by enjoyable reunions with my classmates, of the first twenty years of my life that I lived there. That would be approximately seven thousand three hundred more days than the all-knowing reporter spent there. Except for family members and public figures, names have been changed.

In the Town Where It Happened

Marinette is located at a latitude of 45 degrees, exactly halfway between the North Pole and the equator, although its climate is unlikely to induce thoughts of sweltering heat or tropical breezes. The city is situated at the mouth of the Menominee River as well as on Green Bay, which is part of Lake Michigan. If there had been real estate agents when the town was being settled they would have identified the location as prime property since waterways were the highways of that era, and this town is situated at the intersection two of them. It is thought to have been first settled by Native Americans of the Menominee tribe at around 1680, and in the mid-1700s became a stopping-off point for French Canadian hunters and fur trappers intent on enriching themselves, and missionaries intent on converting and colonizing the region.

Marie Antoinette Chevalier, the daughter of a Canadian and a Native American arrived in the area early in the 1800s and she and her husband built a trading post. She was probably named after Marie Antoinette, queen of France at the time of her birth. After losing her second husband at age forty-six, she developed the trading post by herself into a successful enterprise, and she was widely respected for her business sense, as well as for her ability to deal with people of all types with fairness and respect. She was so highly thought of that she was often called Queen Marinette, and both the city and the county were named in her honor. Any list of counties and county seats both named after the same Native American female would probably be a very short list. Had she been born a decade and a half earlier, when Queen Leszczynskiski ruled France, the name of the town might have been more of a tongue twister.

When you visit Marinette you might drive on Stephenson Street, relax at Stephenson Island Park, and bank at the Stephenson National Bank. If you were to guess that Stephenson was a person of great significance to the community, you would be correct. If still not convinced, look for his statue on Riverside Avenue. Although not born in town, he is thought of as a local boy who made good. Isaac Stephenson, born in Canada, arrived in Wisconsin in 1845 at the age of sixteen, and in Marinette approximately five years later. Since he had begun working in lumbering with his father when he was ten years old, he was by now not only a highly skilled woodsman, but also an entrepreneur. After amassing a fortune through the lumber business, he branched out into finance and eventually into government at the local, state, and federal levels. He served as US senator for one and a half terms, and he was reputed to be the oldest and richest member of the Senate at that time. Marinette benefited greatly from his philanthropies. (When my father was twenty years old, he drove a wagon in the long funeral cortege for Senator Stephenson.)

Lumbering is no longer the major industry that it once was in the area, but it continues to be significant. In both Marinette and its neighboring city Menominee, cleverly referred to as "the twin cities," there is a paper mill operating 24/7 with a sizable workforce. Marinette Marine Company, despite the inland location, builds ships for military and nonmilitary customers. After completion, a ship will sail through four of the five Great Lakes on its way to the St. Lawrence Seaway and, eventually, the Atlantic Ocean. That journey is more than two thousand miles long and takes approximately ten days. There are other industries also, but the area remains more rural than urban.

Marinette County is the third largest of Wisconsin's seventy-two counties in terms of area, but small in population. Known as "America's Dairyland," as you might expect, it has a large cow population. Marinette County is known as the waterfall capital of the state because of its fifteen waterfalls, some of which are in parks, and all of which are available to the public. Menominee County is the eighth largest of Michigan's eighty-three counties in terms of area, but also small in population. Population density is a good indicator of the congestion within an area. Marinette

County has approximately twenty-seven persons per square mile, and Menominee County has twenty-four. For purposes of comparison, Brown County (Green Bay) has 410, and Milwaukee County has 801. In the twin cities there is not only plenty of elbow room, but more than enough space to swing the proverbial cat, not that any resident of Marinette would ever consider doing such a thing. Of Menominee residents, there is some question. There would probably even be space enough to swing a cow if one had the strength and inclination to do so.

The fact that the two towns are of approximately the same size and less than a mile apart guarantees rivalry between them, and representing different states only exacerbates the competitive spirit. All that separates the two towns is a river, which marks the border between the two states, and a bridge, aptly referred to as the "interstate bridge." Their football teams first met in 1894, and the annual game is the oldest interstate rivalry between public schools in the nation. For many years, the "M&M" game was played on November 11, Armistice Day, and all the schools would end classes at noon of that day. On the nights preceding the game, there would be parades, pep rallies, and pranks attempted against the opponent. Large groups of students would hold "snake dances" in which long lines of participants would weave in and out of traffic, thoroughly irritating drivers by disrupting traffic downtown or on the interstate bridge. Most drivers would tolerate such hijinks, perhaps recalling their own youthful exuberance, but there were instances when a driver, overcome with anger, would roll his window down and swear at the celebrants. Although that did not happen often, such glaring misbehavior constituted the most severe form of road rage.

There were occasions when the two states would respond differently to an issue, and it would be border towns like the twin cities that would be most impacted by the repercussions. For example, due to strict rationing during the war most families were rarely able to get butter. A product called oleomargarine was being promoted as a substitute for butter and colored to look like butter. Grocery stores in most states routinely sold it. Wisconsin, however, being the dairy state, insisted that the product not be allowed to masquerade as butter and prohibited the sale of yellow "oleo" in the state. Without coloring oleo looked as appetizing as paste, so the product sold in Wisconsin would come with a plastic capsule of yellow food coloring enclosed. After squeezing the contents of the capsule into the oleo and stirring it vigorously, it would resemble butter. Whether it tasted like butter is still being debated.

Marinette residents had to make a choice. Do they buy the uncolored version, which entailed tedious stirring, or do they break the law and drive across the bridge for the colored product? Many chose to cross the bridge, and some of the risk-takers were apprehended and fined for the infraction. There were instances in which cars loaded with cases of yellow oleo would be stopped by the police and the driver arrested. Those drivers were often headed to a larger city such as Green Bay or Oshkosh with the intent of distributing it to friends, neighbors, or, perhaps selling it. Skirmishes over the butter substitute became known as "the oleo wars." Soon after the real war ended, butter became more available, and the furor subsided; however, it was more than twenty years before Wisconsin allowed the sale of yellow margarine.

Another example of the actions of one state influencing behavior in another state occurred in 1951. When most states switched to daylight saving time, the state of Michigan chose not to do that, and it created confusion in both towns since many people who lived in one town worked in the other. Also, when bars closed in Marinette at 1:00 a.m., it was only midnight in Menominee, and there would be a steady stream of traffic, especially on Fridays and Saturdays, over the bridge with thirsty people intent on one more hour of socialization. Opinions were divided as to whether that was a positive or negative by-product of the daylight saving time fiasco, but Michigan returned to daylight saving time the next year.

The fact that Marinette, a town with an approximate population of 12,000 in 1950, supported twenty-three churches suggest a high level of church membership. The fact that the population was also able to support forty-five taverns is equally impressive. Some people felt that it was the long brutal winters that explained the popularity of neighborhood taverns. Others attributed it to the strong statewide Germanic influence. By most accounts, however, the Irish, French, Germans, Poles, Swedes, Norwegians, and most everyone else enjoyed patronizing their favorite tavern, and some residents had more than one favorite.

Seven miles south of Marinette is the town of Peshtigo. It is less than half the size of Marinette, and is best known as the site of the deadliest fire in US history. It occurred in 1871, on the same day as the better-known Chicago fire; however, the Peshtigo conflagration was much more destructive. In Chicago, the area burned was three and one-half square miles, and approximately 300 people died. The Peshtigo fire devastated 1,800 square miles and killed more than 1,100 people.

Highway 41 is one of the longest north-south highways in the United States, and it cuts though the center of town where it is known as Hall Avenue. A nondescript intersection in downtown Miami, Florida, marks the starting point of the highway, and it continues for more than two thousand miles until it reaches Copper Harbor, Michigan. On a map, it looks like any other road, but to my friends and me it was a highway of dreams. We marveled at the notion that a driver could stay on that one road all the way from often-chilly Marinette, Wisconsin, to balmy Miami, Florida. The fact that none of us knew or even heard of anyone who had ever done that did not stop each of us from identifying that as one of the first things we would do when we grew up. We never speculated about making the two-hundred-mile trip to Copper Harbor, Michigan, the northern end of the highway, since that town would likely bear a strong resemblance to our hometown and furthermore lacked the allure of palm trees and sunny beaches. (As an adult, I have visited Copper Harbor several times, a picturesque town on a peninsula extending into beautiful Lake Superior, and it is well worth the trip.)

Millions of people traveled on Greyhound buses at the time, and my friends and I would marvel at the sleek lines and shiny exterior of the vehicles. Several Greyhounds came through town daily, and a sign on the front of each bus indicated its destination. Names such as Escanaba, Saint Ignace, and Manistique screamed adventure and excitement to us, and traveling by Greyhound was high on our wish list. Since I was in grade school then, during the 1940s, there was plenty of time for marveling and pondering.

Here Comes the Sun

In any ranking of the best years to be born, 1936 would be low on the list. The nation was slowly emerging from the Great Depression, and many people still did not have jobs. Some had been unemployed for more than five years, and prospects did not seem promising.

I was born in November at the M&M Hospital in Marinette, Wisconsin. The second "M" stands for Menominee, Michigan, a town of similar size located one mile north. The hospital was a two-story wooden structure long past its prime. Painted a drab shade of grey, it would have blended in perfectly with a typical November day in northeastern Wisconsin. It was conveniently located one block from our house, so close that my parents could have easily walked to it. Considering the weather, however, they probably drove.

My earliest distinct memories were probably formed around my third birthday. There was a lot of commotion around the house most days since my brother and sister, being close in age, devoted much time to bickering. Pat sometimes tried to boss Mary Lou, but he rarely succeeded since she was never a pushover. She always stood up to him; however, that had little effect on the skirmishes, which were an enjoyable part of their daily routine. I was more of an observer than a participant due to the age difference.

My mother was not bothered by the chaos, and she would step in only when it seemed to be getting out of hand. Pat would occasionally get overly rambunctious, but it was a happy house. We lived our lives to a background of music from the radio. When my father got home from his shop things would quiet down a little and the radio would be turned to the news.

Not only did my mother love music, she also played the piano. While she was in elementary school, her older sister gave her fifty cents each week to pay for her piano lessons. At that time, pianos were a common source of entertainment, and many families had one in their living room. As a young lady, my mother had a clerical job in a music store, and she would also play popular songs for customers who were thinking of buying sheet music. We had an upright piano, of uncertain vintage, in our living room. The piano was white, out of tune, and showed signs of wear, but Mary Lou (I called her Sis), who took piano lessons from fourth through tenth grade, could play it well. I, on the other hand, when offered the opportunity to take lessons would not consider it, mainly because my friends considered it a "sissy" thing to do. I was a sheep in the making.

Being a housewife was a full-time job since there were few laborsaving devices available. Everyone else would be out of the house by 8:00 a.m., but by 10:00, my mother would have to start to prepare the noon meal. We called it "dinner" and it was the main meal of the day. Everyone came home for it. My father's shop was just a half block away, but it was almost a mile to school. Pat and Sis (and later I) made that hike four times every school day. The evening meal, "supper," would be a little lighter, sometimes leftovers from noon. In the afternoon, my mother and I would often walk to the A&P grocery store, which was right down the street, to purchase necessary items. (Remember: we lived in the center of town.)

Although there were always chores waiting to be done, my mother was always upbeat and positive. Most importantly, she found time for me, especially when Pat and Sis were at school. In fact, she probably smothered me with attention and affection as she began to teach me nursery rhymes and songs. The first song I remember is "Playmate, Come Out and Play with Me," and the reason I recall it clearly is because I sang it so often for neighbors and family friends.

Neighborhoods were different back then, and it was common for neighbors to stop by, unannounced, for a short visit. Because of our downtown location, people we knew from school or church might drop in while downtown to shop. Most of the visitors were ladies who were my mother's friends. Sometimes there were snacks, but one thing was certain: visitors to our house would not escape without hearing my rendition of the "Playmate" song. Listeners would gush over my singing. Compliments like "wonderful," "beautiful voice," "like a professional," rained down on me, and I just lapped those compliments up. Most drop-ins came in the afternoon, but if people came in the evening, my dad always enjoyed hearing me. My siblings, however, remained noncommittal on the subject.

Several weeks after I had started performing, it became obvious that I needed new material. Not as many people were dropping by now. They probably had grown tired of hearing the "Playmate" song. They could not possibly be tiring of the singer. At that time, tension was mounting in the United States since the US seemed likely to enter the war, and the times called for a patriotic song. My mother chose "God Bless America," an old song that was growing in popularity. She taught me to sing it with enthusiasm and energy. Unlike the childish "Playmate" song, this was something you could sink your teeth into, and I did just that. My "fans" loved it. In fact, I never got a negative review.

One of my mother's friends considered herself a serious poet, and she would stop in every few weeks. She drove an unusual car that had been built for her by a neighbor. It resembled an oversized golf cart, except that it stood a little higher off the ground because of its larger tires. Its roof was a piece of canvas that was bordered by a red fringe. It had no doors, no windows, no windshield, but it did have a horn—a loud horn that was operated by squeezing a rubber bulb. It was powered by a gasoline engine that made a chugging sound. The car was a dog magnet, and there would always be two or three chasing her car. There were no leash laws at that time, and many dogs roamed freely. People gawked whenever it chugged by with the horn squawking at the darting dogs. When she parked in front of our house, a small crowd would gather, gazing in wonder at the mechanical oddity.

Pat and Sis found her to be hilarious and referred to her as Lizzie Bumstead, but never in her presence. She would come over to chat and to share her latest poem with us. Although her poems are long forgotten, I still remember the dramatic flair she demonstrated in conveying their message. One minute she would be whispering and the next shouting, and through it all I would sit awestruck. The fact that she usually brought candy didn't hurt either, nor did the fact that she always raved about my singing.

There were other songs I learned as we sang along with the radio, but only three that I remember. The third one is "You Are My Sunshine." Gene Autry, one of Hollywood's first singing cowboys popularized it, and for a simple song it conveys many different emotions. It begins with comparing an individual to the sun, a major compliment for sure, and then moves to a plea that the sunshine not be taken away, and ends with the sadness of having lost the sunshine, all in a few short verses. I probably missed some of the subtle nuances in my rendition, but I loved singing it with my mother, and to this day, when I think of her that song is often in my head.

In the 1940s, hats were an important part of every woman's wardrobe. My mother loved hats and enjoyed shopping for them. One day she returned from downtown with a bag containing three hats. Unable to decide which one to buy, she wanted us to select our favorite. She placed the hats on the kitchen table for our consideration, and we proceeded to inspect each hat carefully until Dad told a joke about the hats. Then Pat and Sis chimed in with funny comments, and the next half hour was spent ridiculing the hats. No one laughed more than my mother. The hat she bought the next day was, most likely, the one she had planned to buy right from the start. I believe it was the one that reminded us of a snail.

My father would occasionally reminisce about his school days, when he played basketball for St. Mary's Institute from which he graduated in 1916. (It was later renamed Our Lady of Lourdes School.) The basketball court that the team practiced on was half the size of a conventional one, and in the center of the court was a steel post that supported the roof. The six-inch post was padded, but players would sometimes run into it and regret the encounter. One of their opponents was Sturgeon Bay High School, one hundred miles away by land, but less than twenty miles by water. One night the team was riding to Sturgeon Bay in a horse-drawn sleigh across the frozen water of Green Bay, and the horse fell through the ice. It took a true team effort to extract the horse from the water without anyone else falling in. Although he could not remember which team won the game, the horse would have to be acknowledged as the overall winner. Sometimes my father would render this cheer from those days: "Rooty toot toot. Rooty toot toot. We are the boys from the Institute. We don't cuss and we don't chew, and we don't go with girls who do."

One morning in late summer when Pat went onto the front porch to get our milk, which was delivered daily in glass bottles, he ran back inside saying, "There's a bum with a big beard sleeping on our swing." My mother jumped up to investigate and returned saying, "That man is no bum. He's your uncle Sam." In midafternoon of the same day, a man rushed into my dad's shop, saying, "I just saw your little boy walking around downtown with some Russian," and Dad had to say, "That man's no Russian. He's my brother-in-law." Uncle Sam, my mother's older brother, kept all the kids in the neighborhood entertained with stories of his travels, but after two days he moved on. At that time, there were many rootless people, mostly males without jobs or hope, who traveled around the country by hitchhiking or by riding on freight trains. My dad always referred to Uncle Sam as a "knight of the open road."

Although his visit was brief, Uncle Sam fascinated me and my friends with his stories as well as with his beard, and I was impressed by the fact that he came some distance to visit us. We did not have many relatives in town, so it seemed to me to be quite a special occasion. My father did not share that sentiment. When my friends asked me when Sam would be returning, my father probably hoped that "never" would be the correct answer, and it was. We never saw him again.

Three of my four grandparents died before I was born, and the only one I knew was my father's mother. She lived in a grey stucco house close to my father's blacksmith shop. She was worn down by a hard life raising six boys and one girl, and was a person who saw the glass as mostly empty. She sat in a rocking chair every day, a rosary in her hands, watching the activity around the shop. She disapproved of most aspects of "modern" life, especially how the role of women was changing. The notion of women drinking alcoholic beverages in public scandalized her, as did the growing custom of women wearing pants.

One summer afternoon there was a small parade publicizing a movie, *Badman's Territory* starring Randolph Scott, soon to play at the Fox Theatre. The parade consisted of a covered wagon pulled by two horses and a group of ten cowboys and cowgirls riding horses and carrying banners. Soon after the parade ended, I walked to the shop and was surprised to see four of the riders, two men and two women, with their horses there. They were there because one horse had lost a shoe, and while my father tended to the horse, the riders lounged on a patch of grass alongside my grandma's house, enjoying bottles of beer from Harold's Knight Kap, a nearby tavern.

After work that day, my dad visited his mother, and she had not yet recovered from what she had witnessed. She gave him an earful on the idea of doing business with "that kind of people." Seeing women wearing pants was bad enough. Seeing them drinking beer in public raised it to a new level of decadence. "There is no hope for the future," is not a direct quote, but it does express her sentiment that day and most days

Three months before my fifth birthday I started kindergarten at Ella Court School, a public school housed in an old redbrick building. It was located four blocks away, and I had to walk through the town square to get there. For the first few months, an obliging neighbor would usually walk with me.

There were twenty children in my class, and the teacher's name was Miss Nelson. She was probably in her midtwenties and everyone loved her because she made learning such fun. Kindergarten lasted all day, from 9:00 until 3:00. We each brought a sandwich, and my favorite was bologna with mustard. After lunch, we would take a thirty-minute nap on mats that our mothers had made. My mat was covered with black oilcloth and trimmed with yellow yarn, and it was like a security blanket. I loved everything about kindergarten. Thanks to Miss Nelson, I was confident that I was ready for first grade, assuming there would be naps.

After that, it was on to Our Lady of Lourdes School, which I attended for the next twelve years, and was taught by the School Sisters of Notre Dame. None of the nuns turned out to be quite as sweet as Miss Nelson had been, but I soon felt at home there, even though there were no naps.

Music was a part of the curriculum at school, and every day the music teacher would work with us for twenty or thirty minutes. Some days she would roll a portable organ into our classroom and teach us songs, sometimes hymns. One day, because of a shortage of songbooks, each student was to share a book with another. I, the ultimate rule follower, was told to partner with Earl, the class clown. The teacher probably was hoping that I might serve as a positive influence on Earl. However, when Earl's suggestion that we sing as loud as we could struck me as a good idea, the teacher's hopes were dashed, and never again were we paired.

Sometimes the teacher would give each of us an instrument and we would become a "band," using the term loosely. The most desirable instrument in the band was the tambourine, but there was only one of them. After that came cymbals, bells, rattles, triangles, and drumsticks, which were at the bottom of the status ladder. I was in the half of the class that received drumsticks. Occasionally a student would be moved from one instrument to another, but that was not in my future. I was to remain a "lifer" in the drumstick section, possibly because of the skills I demonstrated with the challenging instrument. The band was intended to teach us the notion of rhythm as well as the different types of rhythm, and we loved that class. I never understood why our primary teacher always left the room when music class began.

Every day at 3:00, a bell would announce the end of the school day. The first-graders would then march to the cloakroom to a scratchy recording of the Notre Dame Victory March. It was a short march since the cloakroom was immediately adjacent to the classroom, but if it was not an orderly march we would have to return to our seats and do it again. "This time with a straight line and no pushing."

The cloakroom was about twenty feet long and four feet wide with a row of clothes hooks on one wall, one hook per student. The room remained neat during those precious few months of mild weather when everyone dressed lightly, however, when winter arrived the appearance of the cloakroom changed dramatically. Instead of lightweight jackets, most of the first-graders would now be dressed in snowsuits with scarves, wool caps, mittens, and rubber boots or galoshes. The clothes hooks might have been perfect for schools in south Florida, but definitely not for northern Wisconsin. Clothing would wind up on the floor in heaps, and finding what was yours would be a daily challenge. It would be reason to celebrate if I arrived home with all the same garments I had worn that morning.

It was in third grade that Sister Pauline became upset with me for talking too much to my classmates when I was supposed to be paying attention to her. She told me that I would be staying after school for my misbehavior, and immediately after the bell sounded she talked to me about the importance of following instructions. She next told me to write "I must obey" one hundred times on the black chalkboard in the front of the room. Not everyone attaches a great deal of importance to spelling.

Napoleon Bonaparte, for example, reportedly felt that a man occupied in important business need not be concerned with proper spelling. Sister Pauline, however, did not share that sentiment or perhaps she felt that my talking did not pertain to "important business." For whatever reason, after I had written the statement one hundred times she made me do it all over again because I had misspelled "obey." Who knew that "obey" did not have an "a" in it? I didn't, at least not until that day. That evening, while playing with my set of Lincoln Logs, I wrote that ill-fated word on every one of the green roofing slats in the set, just so I would never forget the spelling. It worked, although the concept would occasionally elude me.

It's a Blue World

After six months at Lourdes School, I no longer had any pressing concerns regarding school. Not only did I enjoy it, but I looked forward to school each day; however, something had changed at home. On two occasions, I had walked into the house and found my mother crying while talking on the telephone to Mrs. Riley, a friend who lived two houses down from us. Both times she said, "It's nothing, Jimmy. Go in the other room." Having never seen my mother cry before, I knew that it was not nothing.

Unbeknownst to me, my mother had been experiencing pain for some time before she went to the doctor. He told her that she had a thyroid condition, and she would have to have surgery. He assured her that he was able to perform the operation. Dad wanted to take her to Green Bay, fifty miles south, because the doctors were more experienced and the hospital was more modern, but she resisted. She thought that would be too expensive. Besides, her doctor had assured her that he could do the surgery, and she had confidence in him.

The day after the operation, in the afternoon, Mrs. Riley rushed into our house, without even knocking, and said, "Your Mom is in very serious condition. Get down on your knees and pray for her," and we did. That evening Dad told us that Mom had died. Her name was Beatrice King Lahiff, and her friends called her Bea. She was forty-two years old.

It was customary at that time for the wake to be held at the home of the deceased the night before the funeral. Our living room was rectangular, with a bay window facing Ludington Street. The open casket was placed in front of the bay window with curtains closed. There were thirty-five to forty folding chairs set up, and at 7:30 Father Ahearn, our pastor, let the group in saying the rosary. One of my clearest memories from that night was when, during a momentary pause in the group prayers, I asked Uncle Tom to tell me about the hoboes, and people around us laughed. He whispered "later" to me and the prayers resumed. There were not enough chairs for all the mourners, and many stood in adjacent rooms.

Her funeral was held the next morning at Lourdes Church. The date was April 15, 1942, ten days after Easter, and Father Ahearn said the Mass. Early that afternoon my mother was buried at Forest Home Cemetery. By then I grasped the idea that she was up in heaven with the angels since so many people had told me that. It was a few more days before I understood the meaning of "for all eternity."

For the next week, our house throbbed with activity, not only because people kept bringing food over but also because all five of my dad's brothers were in town for the funeral. One already lived here, but the other four and their wives traveled a good distance to come, two from Chicago. All of them stayed at the Hotel Marinette on the town square, one block from our house.

The brothers, my uncles, were close together in age but not in many other respects. They never corresponded, nor did they ever visit one another, but for those few days, they were united in an attempt to lift our spirits. There were many jokes, wisecracks, and funny stories told to us, and all five uncles participated.

My favorite uncle was my dad's older brother, Tom, who worked as a yard boss for the Burlington Railroad in Chicago. In his job he encountered many "hoboes" who had been caught while trying to sneak on or off a freight train, and he had dozens of stories about his experiences with them. He thought that most of them were simply poor, hungry young men, looking for a job. It did not matter if his stories were funny, sad, or exciting; I never tired of hearing them. The life of a hobo struck me as the most glamourous life imaginable.

Neighbors and friends continued to bring us food for a few weeks after our visitors had departed, but those good deeds gradually came to an end. After several weeks of oatmeal for breakfast and sandwiches for lunch, which we called dinner, and also for supper, Dad hired a lady to cook dinner for us five days a week. Her name was Mrs. Timmons, and we soon called her Tim. Not only was she a good cook; she was a very nice person. She would prepare enough food at noon so the leftovers would be our supper, and that system worked well.

At that time radio was my main form of entertainment, and I would listen to thirty-minute dramas for an hour or two every night. One show was about a man who had lost his job, but it was the beginning that impressed me. At the start of the story, the man's boss called him into his office and said some variation of "Well, Jenkins, I don't like the way you've been doing your job. You're fired."

The next day after dinner, while Tim and I were alone in the kitchen, I gave her the bad news. I said "Well, Tim, I don't like your cooking. You're fired." She started crying, and I grew flustered, not knowing what to do next. The radio show had made it seem so simple. Then I reacted just as many managers would have. I walked out of the room. That night when I told my dad what I had done, he simply said, "She'd better be here tomorrow."

At school the next morning, I had trouble concentrating on my work. Ordinarily, I might daydream a little about what we might have for dinner, but that morning all I could think about was who would be there to cook dinner. The walk home at noon was excruciating and seemed to take forever. I opened the door apprehensively expecting the worst, but fortunately for me and my family, Tim was at the stove preparing dinner.

During the next eighteen months, there would be quite a bit of turnover among the ladies who cooked for us. None of them stayed for more than three or four months. It seemed that cooking for us was not exactly a highly coveted job. However, my firing days were over.

In the months following the tragedy, Dad would sometimes drive us to the cemetery to visit mother's grave and to say a prayer. One day he and I stopped for a visit, and he told me to stay in the car because he would only be a minute. When he returned to the car, he folded his arms over the steering wheel, buried his face in his arms, and dissolved into the loudest sobs imaginable. His outburst probably continued for no more than a minute or two, but it seemed much longer to me, sitting alongside of him, frozen in place and not knowing what to do or to say. Losing her changed my family's world in every way. It was as though after having enjoyed bright sunshine every day, you are suddenly exposed to unrelenting days of darkness. Months would pass before occasional rays of sunshine would begin to appear.

Within a week or two of the funeral, Sis began reading a bedtime story to me each night. She read from a thick book containing 365 stories, and we went through that book twice. She would also point out key words to me, and she helped turn me into a reader. She was always there for me, a constant presence trying to light the path forward.

When summer vacation began, after my mother's death, Sis and I rode the Chicago Northwestern 400 to Chicago for a two-week visit with Uncle Tom and Aunt Ethel. The 400 was a new diesel-powered, high-speed express, and we were most impressed. Of course, neither of us had ever been on a train before.

The two weeks sped by as we were kept busy every day. We visited the Brookfield Zoo twice, admired the tall buildings downtown, watched baseball games in a nearby park, and I drank a whole lot of "pop," the midwestern name for soda. So much pop that I could feel it sloshing around in my stomach when I walked. I vowed to go on the wagon after this trip.

Tom and Ethel lived in a spacious two-story redbrick house in Western Springs, a Chicago suburb. If you went out the front door at 5:59 p.m., walked to the sidewalk, and turned to the right, you would see two blocks away, precisely at 6:00 p.m., the Silver Streak Zephyr, the flagship train of the Burlington fleet, as it headed for Los Angeles.

One day Aunt Ethel took us downtown to see the railroad yard where Tom worked as a yard boss. I had hoped to meet, or at least see, some hoboes there, but that didn't happen; however, Tom had arranged for Sis and I to ride in the cab of the Silver Streak as the train was about to depart for Los Angeles. The railroad yard was huge so the trip was probably two or three miles, and during that time the engineer showed us how to operate the train. He braked the train at the yard's exit, and we were lifted back to the ground and each given an engineer's cap. Then the engine roared and the train began its westward journey. The Silver Streak probably didn't get to Western Springs until 6:01 that night, but there was a good excuse.

Our last night at Tom's coincided with an air raid drill in the Chicago metropolitan area. World War II was raging, and the public had been made aware of the possibility of air attacks. Radio stations had been alerting listeners to the upcoming drill ever since we had gotten to Chicago, and even I was aware of the dos and don'ts of surviving an air raid, as well as the importance of maintaining a complete blackout. The practice raid would last from 8:00 until 9:00, and I was excited. This would be my first drill.

Sis and I were in the living room along with Lucy, our twenty-year-old cousin, and her boyfriend when the magic hour arrived. For the tenth time, I inspected each window shade to make sure that it was pulled down as far as possible, and then I shut the ceiling light off. The room was now in total darkness in perfect compliance with instructions. The patriotic fervor that engulfed the entire nation, however, had somehow missed Lucy. It was probably 8:01 when she said, "This is so stupid" and lit the first of many cigarettes. Trying to be helpful, I told her that smoking was prohibited during air raids and reminded her that a highly trained pilot is able to detect the glow of a cigarette from thousands of feet up in the sky. It was all to no avail. That night I learned that some people don't appreciate advice, no matter how well-intended it may be. While Lucy smoked cigarette after cigarette, pausing occasionally to make a sarcastic comment, I sat there certain that some highly trained German pilot was about to detect the glow from Lucy's cigarette and bombs would rain down on us. Somehow, we avoided disaster that night, and the next day, unscathed, we rode the 400 back home.

When we got home, I immediately told Dad and Pat about the excitement of the air-raid drill. I informed them about the rules that had to be followed and even explained why those rules were so important. My father must have been quite impressed because the next day when he came home from work, he had a brand new air-raid warden helmet for me. It was bright red with a badge on the front and a black chin strap. (See last page.) That became my headpiece of choice for the entire summer.

Praise the Lord and Pass the Ammunition

Several weeks after our Chicago trip it was announced that Marinette would soon have a practice air drill, and our local newspaper, the *Eagle-Star*, listed the names of all the block wardens for the entire city. The warden for our block was Mr. McGill, an older retired man who lived three houses down from us, and within minutes I was knocking on his front door. I told him about my recent experience in an air-raid drill, and he was obviously impressed. The official air-raid warden helmet that I was wearing most likely enhanced my credibility even more. I told him that I would be available for duty. He thanked me for offering my services and assured me that he would phone me if assistance were needed.

My house was on a block that was a combination of residential and commercial properties. In addition to the five houses on our block, there was a Scott Paper warehouse, a printing shop, an A&P grocery, a taxi stand, and a Standard Oil gas station. Across the street were two apartment houses, two single-family homes, a Shell gas station, and a parking lot. Behind our house was a road that led to the "yacht basin" and the radio station. We truly lived in center city Marinette. As air-raid warden for our block, Mr. McGill had significant responsibilities. Considering his age and my extensive experience, I was certain that he would have the wisdom to rely on me. After all, he had never even been through a practice air-raid drill.

On the night of the drill, I first inspected our house to be sure that it was in compliance with the rules and then made sure that neither Pat nor

Sis was smoking. Pat was twelve and Sis eleven, but a warden should never take anything for granted.

I positioned myself closest to the phone so I would be able to pick it up after the first ring just as the urgency of the situation would demand. Dial telephones had not yet come to my town, and all calls were made with the assistance of an operator who would ask, "Number, please?" and then make the desired connection. Twice I lifted the receiver to be sure that the phone was in working order. The second time the operator told me not to pick it up if I didn't intend to make a call. I tried to explain the seriousness of the situation to her, but she said that if I lifted it up a third time she would report me to her supervisor. Until then I had never believed the stories about how nosy and bossy telephone operators were and how they would always listen in on other peoples' phone calls, but that experience turned me into a skeptic. She didn't sound very patriotic either.

On December 7, 1941, Japan attacked the US naval base in Honolulu, Hawaii, and the US entered the war. It would be three and a half years before the Allies won it. Throughout those three and a half years, everyday life was transformed in many different ways. Products such as gasoline, tires, meat, and butter were rationed and could only be bought in limited quantities based on the number of government stamps issued to your family. Towns conducted "scrap drives" in order to collect materials such as iron, tinfoil, nylon, rubber, fat, and cooking oil, which would be converted into products for military use. All these activities were a part of the "defense effort."

It would be impossible to exaggerate how involved the people of this nation were in World War II. Most knew someone who had been drafted or enlisted into military service. Several of the nuns had brothers or uncles fighting overseas, and they would often talk about the letters that their family had received from them. For security purposes, military personnel serving overseas were not allowed to reveal where they were, and their letters would be censored before being mailed. References to specific locations would be scissored out of the letter so relatives would be left to speculate as to their whereabouts. Two of my uncles were drafted into the army. Marcus was assigned to an army base in the States for the duration of the war, and Wilbert, often called Pat, served in the Pacific campaign against the Japanese. He was hospitalized for two weeks with malaria.

Since I envisioned him being awarded medals and citations on a weekly basis, I wrote him a letter asking him to send me one of his medals, and he did. Although I never did learn the reason he received the medal, I was proud of it.

It was important to conserve food so that our country could provide for our troops overseas as well as to help the millions of Europeans who were starving. That was why my class joined the Clean Plate Club. We signed a pledge to never take more food than we could eat and to always clean our plate. Every signee was given a pin and a membership card that identified them as a member of this select group, and I wore my pin proudly. After six months, I lost my pin, but I adhered to the Club's creed until the war ended. At the start of the war, I disliked lima beans, which we had frequently. By war's end, dislike had turned to outright hatred. I have not eaten one since. However, I contributed to the defense effort by eating lima beans.

When school resumed after Christmas vacation, it was announced that there would be an assembly the next day for grades one through eight. Since assemblies had always been announced a week in advance, I figured that this must be special. The next morning when I got to school and saw four soldiers standing near the main entrance, I knew it was really special.

The soldiers described for the assembly the tremendous obstacles our country faced in fighting our enemies and how each and every person must do their part. I was ready to enlist, but what they wanted us to do was to buy US savings stamps to help the war effort. Then they brought a model jeep onto the stage. It was half the size of the real version but identical in all other details.

The soldiers droned on for fifteen minutes about the savings stamp program, but they had lost the attention of the males in the lower grades who were mesmerized by the grandeur of the model jeep. At the conclusion of the program, when the speaker announced that the model jeep would remain at our school as a reminder to buy savings stamps, a cheer went up from the boys of grades one through four.

The model jeep would be the center of attention for the next two months. It was placed in the main lobby, and there was a heavy rope fence set up around it to keep admirers from touching it. The day after the jeep's arrival, the principal announced that there was to be a competition

JAMES LAHIFF

between grades one through four, and one lucky member of the class that bought the most savings stamps would win the model jeep.

One savings stamp cost ten cents, and we were each given a small booklet in which to paste them. A booklet had spaces for about 190 stamps. When it was full, you would exchange it for a US Savings Bond at a bank, and in ten years the bond would be worth twenty-five dollars. Sister Anne explained all these important details to the class several times, but she recognized daydreaming when she saw it and knew that the odds of getting through to us were against her.

The contest was intended to motivate us to do our part and help the defense effort by buying savings stamps, but it was the possibility of winning the jeep that fired us up. My class had to beat the other three classes and thereby give one classmate, preferably me, a shot at winning the prize. And a wonderful prize it was with its army-green finish, buffed to such a sheen that it mirrored anyone who stopped to gaze at it, as I did as often as possible.

This competition made me a changed person. In the past, I had occasionally run errands for a neighbor when asked to do so. Now running errands became my mission in life and every day after school I would stop at Mrs. McGill's to see if I could be of service. Frequently, she would send me up the street to the A&P for some groceries and she would tip me five cents. Occasionally the errand was to the post office, and the tip would be a dime. My dad would give me a few dimes also so when my class lined up at the principal's office on Friday afternoon to buy stamps, I would be able to buy five or six.

Each Monday afternoon the principal made it seem like a horse race when she announced the standings in the savings stamp's marathon. The four classes were similar in size, about twenty-five students each, and similar in the number of stamps being purchased. The race was truly neck and neck. Whenever I went over to Mrs. McGill's, I would update her on the race and remind her how important this was for our national defense, and I was sometimes able to squeeze a few extra nickels out of her.

Since my class, second grade, had been in first or second place for the entire two months, I was mildly confident on the Friday when the competition ended. However, we had to wait until Monday to learn the outcome, and the weekend dragged by. I had been mentioning this race in my bedtime prayers for the past eight weeks, and I added a little more pressure over the weekend just to be safe.

At last Monday arrived. Since the principal always waited until 1:00 to make the announcements, the morning seemed to be at least ten hours long. It is well known that the School Sisters of Notre Dame are excellent teachers who care deeply for their students. One of their less recognized skills is the ability to "keep the pot boiling" and thereby let the tension build. True to form, the principal came on the intercom and led off by talking about tomorrow's fire drill, next week's science fair, and a few other unimportant topics. Then she wasted a few more precious minutes by thanking practically everyone in the world for their role in the defense effort.

Finally, the main event. Our top competitor throughout the eight-week contest had been the third grade. Each class had a distinct personality and, unlike the second grade, which was perfect in every way, the third grade was cursed with a cantankerous mindset. On bad days they were extremely churlish, and on better days merely grouchy. If they ever experienced a good day, they would not let it show. For eight weeks, they had been bragging about how they would be the champion. They were "trash talking" long before that term was even coined. When it was announced that the third grade had taken second place, my class erupted in cheers, but we were quickly brought back to earth when Sister said, "Get out your arithmetic books." Although there was still one obstacle to overcome, I was already envisioning the jeep in my living room. A raffle to be held in my class on Friday would determine the winner.

Never during the last eight weeks of bedtime prayers did I mention my ultimate goal. Instead, I had always emphasized how hard the second-grade class was working to aid the defense effort and how much it deserved the championship. I made these same points again and again, hoping that repetition would wear down any possible reluctance.

Now that my class had accomplished its goal, I thought that a more subtle approach might be in order. Each night I thanked God for his help, and in an "Oh, by the way" moment I would mention the upcoming raffle and how wonderful life would be if I were to win the prize. I may have also mentioned that I was a motherless child, but I am not sure that I went that far.

Friday finally came, and shortly after the noon break Sister Anne announced that it was time for the raffle. She brought out a paper bag filled with small folded slips of paper, one for each student. Twenty-four of the slips were blank, and one was marked with a letter X. The person who selected the slip with the X would win the highly coveted model jeep. Several times she warned us not to unfold our paper until everyone in the class had theirs and, holding the bag too high for us to look down into it, she walked between the rows of students while we each reached up and in for the winner.

The moment I selected a slip of paper out of the bag I felt a surge of power course through my body. It was a feeling I had never experienced before nor since. It was a once-in-a-lifetime shock, but there was not a doubt in my mind. I knew immediately that I had won. Sister then busied herself at her desk for a minute or two, allowing the excitement level to rise, and while most of the class sat hoping that they would win, I sat thinking about the fun I was going to have with my new jeep. When told to unfold our slips, I was probably looking quite blasé but feeling overjoyed.

At the end of the day, I went to the principal's office to collect my prize and she told me that Patrick and Mary Lou had "volunteered" to help me carry the jeep home. Although I was only in second grade, I knew that students rarely volunteered for anything but were simply told to do it; however, I was not about to quibble over semantics with such an important task at hand.

Until that moment, I had not given any thought to the logistical issues of carrying this cumbersome prize home, almost a mile away. In exchange for their help, I volunteered to carry their books. I got the better of that deal since Pat, as usual, was not taking any books home and Sis's load was a light one.

The model, half the size of a real jeep, was constructed of heavy cardboard. Although it was not a backbreaker, it was not light either and it proved to be awkward to carry. The walk home took three times longer than usual, and much of the time was spent by the "volunteers" bickering over how to carry it. The most efficient way would require Sis and Pat to both put their heads up into the jeep's body and bear its weight on their shoulders. The problem with this approach would be that neither would be able to see where they were going. I assured them that I could be their guide and warn them of every possible obstacle, but after almost bumping into a lady pushing a baby carriage, they lost confidence in my navigational skills. While they couldn't agree on how best to bear this burden, my mind was elsewhere. I was envisioning the weeks, months, and even years of fun in store for me with my new jeep.

The jeep was placed in a corner of the living room that gave me a good view of the people passing by on the sidewalk, and I spent most of my waking hours that first weekend in my jeep. During the next week, I divided my time between playing with the jeep and playing with friends in the neighborhood. On Monday, the jeep got 80 percent of my attention and my friends got only 20 percent. As the week progressed, I grew more aware of some of the jeep's shortcomings, especially the steering wheel that did not turn and cardboard tires that did not roll. Those two factors will limit one's mobility every time. By Friday, my friends were getting 90 percent of my time. The jeep mysteriously disappeared a few days later, and no one even mentioned it, not even I. That was a good lesson for me on the difference between perception and reality.

Although I no longer had a jeep, my arsenal remained fully stocked. Since this was wartime, many of the most popular toys were military related. My personal armory included a B-17 bomber with a two-feet wingspan, two small tanks, a bazooka, and a squad of ten lead soldiers, each four inches tall. One of my favorite board games was "Commandos Strike at Dawn."

We played war games outdoors almost every day in the neighborhood, and my weapon of choice was a wooden M1 rifle. Three feet long, with a moveable bolt, and a strap for slinging over the shoulder, I never entered battle without it, and I usually carried it while making routine patrols on my block. A frequent impediment to our war games was the fact that no one wanted to be a German soldier. Everyone wanted to be an American, and it took intense negotiating to persuade half the participants to be German "just this once." Once a game began, the disgruntled Germans would often claim to be shot almost immediately, thus ending the game. We would then usually revert to a game of cowboys and Indians (Native Americans) because that required no negotiations. In either setting, however, my M1 always served me well.

JAMES LAHIFF

As the government mobilized for the huge challenge that it faced there was a severe shortage of welders, and my father was asked to teach welding at the local vocational school. He had been welding, both gas and electric, for about fifteen years at that time, and he wound up teaching two three-hour classes every Monday and Wednesday for the next three years. Welders were in great demand.

Jobs were plentiful for welders, especially in shipbuilding and manufacturing. Many welders trained by my father went to work right in town at Marinette Marine, a company started in the late 1930s by two men building fishing boats out of white pine lumber. The first ships produced locally for the government were made of wood, but the company soon transitioned from wood to metal. Any local welder wishing to move to a more exotic locale could easily find work at either of the two shipyards in Sturgeon Bay building patrol boats or in Manitowoc, where submarines were being built. If they really wanted to get away, manufacturing plants in Milwaukee or Chicago were other options.

Prior to the war my father had worked from 8:00 a.m. until 5:00 p.m., but with his new part-time job he would come home at 5:00, wash up, eat supper, and speed to the vocational school where he worked from 6:00 until midnight. His pay could not have been much because he never earned more than $5,000 per year in his lifetime.

It was a mild Sunday afternoon in May 1943, when the Marinette Marine Company launched the first two of five ships that were being built for the government, and I was excited to witness the event. Bands from both public high schools played and flags and banners waved in the breeze. My level of excitement cooled slightly as several prominent individuals gave speeches marking the occasion, but the actual launching made it all worthwhile. The ships, built of lumber from the local area, were 192 feet long and capable of carrying 1,400 tons of cargo. Both of the ships, not surprisingly, were at the edge of the river, and each was held in place by seven ropes, each two inches thick. Seven axe-wielding men stood ready to sever the ropes, and the cuts had to be made simultaneously to assure a smooth launch. When an order was shouted out, the ropes were cut and the first ship, *White Pine I*, slid sideways down the oily ramp. It hit the river with a splash as loud as an explosion and appeared to almost tip on to its side before being righted through the efforts of workers pulling on heavy ropes to secure it. I had optimistically assumed that the second ship would be launched immediately after the first, but there were more speakers to be heard. When the second ship, *White Pine II*, was finally launched it was as dramatic and exciting as had been the launch of its predecessor. We left immediately afterward, even though there were a several more speakers anxious to be heard. My sense of patriotism and confidence in a US victory soared to new heights after having witnessed the contributions to the war effort. If our enemies only knew about today's additions to our fleet, I was sure they would surrender immediately.

The first five ships built by Marinette Marine, referred to as the "White Pine Fleet," were classified as barges because they were ships without power. They were designed to be towed by tugs. The shipyard was operating long hours each day and was able to complete the five ships in less than six months, well ahead of schedule.

The company's next government contract was for six ocean-going tugs, and the first three were launched on schedule. Construction of the final three tugs was slowed by the failure of vital materials to arrive according to plan, and the launch was delayed for several days. The new schedule called for the three tugs to be launched the same day, and all who watched the event came away impressed. The crowd was sparse, with little jostling among the spectators for a better vantage point, no bands, and no long-winded speakers. It was Christmas Eve afternoon. The temperature hovered near zero, and there were blustery winds. The ice on the river was eight inches thick. Workers had spent the morning using steel wrecking bars to break up the ice, and a crane lifted large sections of ice on to the ground in an attempt to provide adequate space for the ships to float. As soon as a tug was launched, workers would board it and continue the fitting operations required for maritime duty. The ceremony began at 2:45 with a brief invocation, followed by equally brief remarks by one of the company's founders, and the launchings were flawless. The three tugs were in the water, and the ceremony concluded at 3:45.

The class was roused from its usual early afternoon stupor on the day that it was announced that a captured Japanese submarine would be on display on Dunlap Square during the upcoming weekend. It was hard to believe that one of those sleek, long vessels like the ones I had seen in *Crash Dive* and *We Dive at Dawn*, had somehow made it to my hometown and, as it turned out, none had. The captured vessel was a two-man submarine, unlike anything I had ever seen in the movies or newsreels. Approximately one-third the length of a standard sub, it was being carried on a flatbed trailer across the US to urge people to buy more US savings bonds.

There was a raised wooden platform, running the length of the sub with steps at both ends, and there was a long line of people patiently waiting to get a closer look. When a person finally got on to the platform, they seemed to do two things: they knocked on the wall with their knuckles, and then they would kick it, as a potential buyer might do with the tires of a car they were thinking of buying. Since the sub did not have any windows, it was not until a person got to the middle of the ship that they could peer down through the open hatch to glimpse the interior. Everyone agreed that it was solidly built, but extremely cramped inside. According to the sailor accompanying the exhibit, the interior temperature would soar to over a hundred degrees when the hatch was closed, making it like a sauna. That bit of information sealed the deal for us. We agreed that serving on a regular submarine would be great, but the two-man version was not for us.

While the war affected the life of every citizen in some way every single day, we also found time for games that were not war-related but could be brutal in the way we played them. On a summer day, four or five kids could start a game of Monopoly that might continue into a second day. When that happened, the position of banker was most important. If Sis were playing, she would be the unanimous choice to be banker since no one ever questioned her competence nor honesty. Anyone else in the role of banker would be viewed with suspicion, oftentimes for good reason. A person might end the first day owning Boardwalk and Park Place, and the next day be informed that they actually owned Baltic and Mediterranean. When Sis was not playing, the second day would often end prematurely with vows to never play again. Two or three days later, another game of Monopoly would commence with virtually the same combatants.

Chinese checkers was another popular game both in our house and in the neighborhood. It was a game in which fortunes could change quickly. One minute you are on the path to an easy win, and the next your predicament is hopeless. For a serious player the game could be frustrating, and we were serious players. We usually played on a rickety card table, and more than once a disgruntled participant stood up and "accidently" knocked the checkerboard to the floor, sending the marbles in all directions and thus ending the game.

Besides being kind, modest, and hardworking, my father was also frugal. Naturalist Henry David Thoreau, who said, "The man is richer whose pleasures are the cheapest," would have approved of him. My father considered the ability to save money one of the most important traits a person could possess. He attempted to instill that trait in his children in many ways. "Quick. Don't let the heat out," was a regular admonition on cold days when someone departing might pause for a moment with the outside door partially open. He would also remind anyone who left a lamp on in an empty room that they were wasting electricity. If a water faucet was left dripping, the guilty party would hear about it.

To anyone who talked on the phone longer than my father thought appropriate, he would say, "That's enough. Don't tie up the line." At that time our family shared the telephone line with another family. It was called a "party line," and it cost less than a single-family line. When you picked up the phone, you might sometimes hear another conversation. You would be unable to make your call until the other party completed their call and hung the phone up. It seemed to me that the other family "tied up" the line much more than we did.

I was told to hang the phone up immediately if I heard someone else talking, but sometimes it was hard to resist listening in on a stranger's call, especially if I was alone in the room. I had already listened to enough detective dramas on nighttime radio to realize that many crimes had been solved or even prevented when a good citizen overheard a phone call. I felt that I was simply practicing good citizenship, but my efforts were never successful. I imagined myself overhearing spies exchanging war secrets. Instead, I would hear, "Yes, we're having the scalloped cabbage, spaghetti, and cheese casserole for dinner again. Harvey says that he could eat it every day." Instead of hearing, "This is Rocky. Meet me the at the club in an hour to plan tomorrow's bank robbery," I would hear, "Bill, how about giving me a ride to work tomorrow? The old jalopy broke down again." I eventually became so disgusted that when I intercepted another's phone call I hung up immediately.

For a long time, my father had been concerned about my weight or lack thereof, and he often talked about the need to "put some meat on his bones." Pat said that when I stood with a bottle of cherry soda in my hand I looked like a thermometer, but he did have a tendency to exaggerate. I was beyond svelte, however, and I heard "bag of bones" more than once. No matter how much I ate my weight remained unchanged. My father's friend Clarence, a pharmacist, suggested that fish oil capsules might solve the problem, so my father went to Sears Roebuck and ordered an economy size bottle. Going to Sears Roebuck did not require much exertion since its back door was a stone's throw from our house and half that distance from the shop.

A week later my father came home with a large bottle of fish oil emulsion capsules, the intended elixir for my weight problem. In the not-so-distant future words like skinny and scrawny would no longer describe my body. I had already vowed to myself that I would stop taking the capsules as soon as my body approached the chubby stage. When my father handed me the first capsule I popped it into my mouth and effortlessly washed it down with a small amount of water. Several weeks would pass before I would be able to repeat that feat. I remember a capsule as being two inches long, but one inch is probably closer to the truth. Time will distort memory, which explains how the fish that got away will grow longer with each retelling of the story. Nonetheless, the capsules were big, the smell terrible, and I could not swallow them.

It would be two weeks before I would swallow another capsule, and during that time I became a master of subterfuge. The plan was for me to take a capsule at breakfast, and each morning there would be one on the table next to my plate. Most mornings everyone would be in a hurry and not notice, and I would surreptitiously put the capsule into my pants pocket. If someone might be watching, I would put the capsule into my mouth take a drink of water or milk, swallow the liquid, and keep the capsule in my mouth until I was able to relocate it to my pocket. From Charlie Chan movies I had learned well the art of deception. On the way to school, I would throw the capsule down through the sewer grate by the Scott warehouse. I had developed a perfect system, and because I was able to outsmart everyone, I had reason to feel smug.

One night, right after supper, my father told me that he had to talk to me. When he lowered the volume on the radio, I knew that it was serious because he attached great importance to staying current with the war news. It turned out that a man had stopped at the shop when his shift at Scott ended at 2:30 that day and told my father that he had seen me throw a pill into the sewer. The windows at the warehouse were permanently frosted, impossible to see through, but this snitch had decided to take an unauthorized smoke break. He opened one of the awning-like windows on the second floor, the one right above the sewer, the scene of the crime, and I had not noticed him. Caught by someone who himself was participating in an unauthorized activity made it especially galling.

When the news program ended, my father turned the radio off and gave me a five-minute tutorial on how to swallow a pill. He then had me swallow three capsules, one at a time, just to show that I could do it. In bed that night I worried about the weight I was likely to gain from my capsule overdose, but in the morning my trousers were as baggy as ever, and my swallowing problems were history. As I was walking to school that morning, a man was leaning out of a second floor window at Scott and smoking a cigarette. When he saw me, he laughed and waved. I assumed he was yesterday's culprit and responded with my most half-hearted wave. I saw no point in encouraging such a lowlife. For the next few weeks, I walked on the other side of the street.

Comic books often carried advertisements for Charles Atlas (birth name Angelo Siciano) and his "Dynamic Tension" bodybuilding course, and his message seemed to be aimed directly at me. Drawn as a comic strip, the story progressed from a scene of a scrawny boy and a pretty girl enjoying themselves on a beach until a masculine bully comes along and kicks sand in the boy's face and humiliates him. The boy goes home, kicks a chair in frustration, and signs up for the Atlas course. After completing the course, the boy, now much more studly, beats up the bully and wins his girlfriend back. The headline of the advertisement would ask, "Are you tired of sand being kicked in your face?" The bodybuilding course was designed for "the 97-pound weakling." In other words, for me, although I had never had sand kicked in my face, perhaps because I spent little time at the beach. "I can make you a new man in only fifteen minutes a day" was the promise that motivated me to order the "free book."

Mail was delivered twice each weekday and once on Saturday, and it was only after thirty-five deliveries that the "book" finally arrived. "Pamphlet" or "booklet" might have been a more accurate description, but if Charles Atlas wanted to call it a book, few people would be likely to argue with him, much less ridicule him for his mistake. The information in the book was evenly divided between reasons for ordering the course and the amazing body changes one could expect from taking the course, which consisted of twelve lessons and one final "perpetual lesson." It struck me as a genuine bargain, all that for only thirty dollars cash or thirty-five dollars credit. I realized, however, that my father would be as likely to join the Lutheran church as to give me that amount of money for a bodybuilding course, even one that promised a "New He-Man Body." He probably would have chuckled at the idea and would have pointed out the many things I could do at the shop to build my muscles. I decided to let that slumbering canine snooze. If there had been a course or a book explaining how the scrawny boy got the pretty girl in the first place, I might have pushed harder for it.

Mr. Atlas proved to be a person who did not accept rejection readily, and he continued to send me letters that always began with "Dear Friend." He seemed genuinely concerned that he had not heard from me and included another order form in case I had mislaid the original. I thought that was very decent of him. In another letter, he worried that my priorities might have gotten jumbled, and later he warned me not to allow bad habits to become a part of my life. After four or five letters, I no longer heard from "my friend" except for an occasional postcard asking me if I had grown tired of having sand kicked in my face.

Beginning to See the Light

Although I do not remember the name of the first movie I ever saw, I was five years old at the time and Sis took me to see it at the Fox Theatre. It was probably a musical since she liked them so much, and movie musicals were at their height of popularity in the 1940s. The country was slowly emerging from the Great Depression while girding itself for war, and the public flocked to movie musicals for their feel-good stories and happy endings. She took me to Sunday matinees occasionally, and it would be either a musical or a Disney story. It was at the Fox that I was introduced to such luminaries as Dumbo, Bambi, and Pinocchio. Sis instilled in me an appreciation of movies that continues today.

While Sister Monica labored to introduce the mysteries of the Holy Trinity to the class, I had already succumbed to the trinity of the Fox, the Rialto, and the Strand. All three theatres were downtown, a short walk from our house, and the price was right. A ticket for a child (up to age twelve) cost twelve cents and a refreshment—Coke, popcorn, or candy—cost five cents. Tickets were even cheaper at the Menominee Opera House, which had been converted into a movie theatre. A child's ticket cost only nine cents, but it would usually require a bus to get there at a cost of five cents each way. It would take a special occasion, such as Free Popcorn Day, for us to make the trip.

At about age seven Saturday matinees with friends became a regular event, and often we would repeat the experience on Sunday afternoon. Saturday matinees usually featured cowboy movies, but the offerings on Sunday would be more sophisticated. Abbott and Costello, the Bowery Boys, and the Three Stooges were always well-received. For the price of admission, you would see two feature films (a "Double Feature"), a five-minute cartoon, "News of the Day," which was a brief summary of that week's news, and a "Preview of Coming Attractions." Early on, we became aware of one critical problem for which there was no vaccine: premature snack consumption (PSC). By the time the movie finally began, we had already consumed all of our snack. After some discussion, we made a pact that none of us would begin to eat until the name of the movie's director appeared on the screen. As every devoted moviegoer knows, the director's name always comes last, at the end of a long list of credits that might include names of the grip, hair stylist, animal wrangler, and many others. A downside of that approach was that if our snack were popcorn, it would be stone-cold by the time we dove into it, but tasty, nonetheless. A victory for delayed gratification. There would be a five minute intermission between the two feature films during which anonymous animated characters would sing, "Let's all go to the lobby to get ourselves a treat" and, anyone who had the money, did just that. The entire show would last three hours or so, and it would be time well spent.

The Saturday matinee experience was completely different from that of a Sunday matinee. The moviegoers on Sunday were a little older and much less demonstrative. They came to watch the movie and, except for an occasional chuckle or slight gasp, there would be very little response to the action on the movie screen. Saturday's crowd, on the other hand, came to participate in the movies, which were usually westerns. The actions of the hero would be applauded as long as he behaved like a hero. There was a rigid code of standards, however, when it came to singing, as Roy Rogers or Gene Autry too often did. Any singing directed at a woman, whether a cowgirl or the school marm, would be greeted with booing and sarcastic remarks; however, singing to the cowhands around a campfire on the prairie was more acceptable. There might be a few groans, but the usual response was one of muted indifference. These discriminating moviegoers seemed to feel that singing to one's horse or cattle herd was completely acceptable.

The villain, dressed in dark clothing, was viewed with contempt and derision, and spectators would comment loudly throughout the proceedings. On several memorable Saturdays the movie stopped, the lights came on, and the manager walked onto the stage and addressed the audience. He scolded us for making too much noise and urged us to behave as we would if we were with our parents. If we did not quiet down, he warned that he would end the matinee. After the film resumed there would be an eerie silence for the next five minutes, and then a single comment would trigger a return to normal.

As an added inducement to lure kids to the Saturday matinee and to keep them coming back, the Fox would often include a serial, ten or twelve short films that would be shown on successive Saturdays. Each episode would end with the hero or heroine facing an incredible predicament, one that would require the young movie buffs to return each Saturday, if only to witness the outcome. Imagine that Tarzan "King of the Jungle" appeared to be in control of the evil-doers as they struggled in the deep jungle, but suddenly he finds himself backed up to a bottomless chasm with the criminals closing in. When the situation looked most hopeless, the episode would end. The following Saturday's episode would briefly reshow the dire situation, and then you might hear the distinctive high pitched hoot of Cheeta, Tarzan's fiercely loyal chimpanzee, and you knew that things would be fine. Cheeta would swing across the deep divide, on a sturdy vine that both would use to escape certain death, and after a deep sigh of satisfaction, you would anticipate the next crisis, due in approximately five minutes.

Walking home after the movie, we were more likely to discuss the serial than either of the feature films since westerns, while always engaging and entertaining, were quite predictable. We were as enthralled with Cheeta as with Tarzan, and often speculated as how great it would be to have a chimpanzee as a pet. That suggestion never generated much conversation at home, undoubtedly because the only tree in our yard was a sapling and there were no vines. During my five or six years of faithful matinee attendance a wide variety of serials were presented. Others that were especially popular were "Jungle Jim" and also "Nyoka the Jungle Girl." Moviegoers from the land of the "frozen tundra" seemed to be attracted to stories set in the hottest jungles of Africa, especially if crocodiles and snakes were included.

Although I usually attended movies with neighborhood friends, there was one time that I went alone. The movie was *Dillinger*, the story of one of the most notorious and well-publicized criminals in modern US history.

When my friend Larry's mother told him that he couldn't go because she did not want her son turned into a criminal that probably summed up the reason none of the others were available, but that strengthened my resolve to see it. Any movie that could turn a classic rule-follower into a criminal had to be seen. Fortunately, at my house there was always more interest in who I was going with than in what the movie was, so I concocted a story about intending to meet someone from school there. I promised myself that if any point I felt myself beginning to harbor any evil impulses, I would leave the theatre immediately, but I was able to see the movie through to its completion. The fact that John Dillinger was able to escape from a county jail by pretending that a small piece of scrap wood was a pistol impressed me greatly. I filed that idea away in my "For Emergency Use Only" mental file.

At that time newspapers were the public's main source of information, and they were widely read and relied upon. During the war years, we subscribed to the *Chicago Tribune*, which modestly advertised itself as "The World's Greatest Newspaper." The "Trib" had great photos of the battlefields, and I always read Arch Ward's "In the Wake of the News" in the sports section. The *Marinette Eagle-Star* was delivered to our house by a boy on a bicycle every late afternoon except Sunday, and I was most interested in the sports pages and the movie advertisements. All three theatres advertised every day and each theatre changed features twice a week so it was a challenge to keep up with current offerings. One day the ad for the Strand was slightly smaller than usual and the next week it had shrunk even more. This trend continued for several weeks until the ad simply said "Closed." The sequence of shrinking notices was like the proverbial canary in the coal mine, but it flew over my head and I was dismayed by the news.

It is true that the Strand had few redeeming qualities. It was the oldest, smallest, and most poorly maintained of the three theatres, and probably in violation of multiple safety codes, but it was the closest to our house. We could see the back of the building from our front door, and I was surprised how quickly the building was demolished. For some unknown reason, I had assumed that a new Strand would be built to replace it, but no such luck.

A one-story office building was constructed in the location, and the front office, facing Main Street, was occupied by an elderly lawyer who was reputed to be crusty and generally grumpy. He had owned a parrot for almost twenty years and he kept it in a cage in his office. The parrot was widely known for its extensive vocabulary of swear words and for its ability to piece those words together. The lawyer claimed not to have any idea of where it had learned such bad words, and if a female or a child entered the office, he would throw a black cloth over the cage to silence it. Any male who entered was fair game for a verbal attack, and there was a good chance that the bird would tell the man where he should go. I never had a reason to enter, but walked past it many times and would often stop and look through the large glass window at the parrot. When the bird was quiet, it would stand erect with a military bearing and a pompous air. It seemed to be very pleased with itself and its bright green plumage. On several occasions, it hunched over, looked directly at me, and seemed to address me. The window glass prevented me from hearing its message and my lip reading skills were not yet developed, but I never had the feeling that the bird was urging me to have a great day.

With the number of local theatres reduced to two I worried that there might no longer be enough suitable movies available for discriminating moviegoers, but that did not turn out to be a problem. Perhaps fewer options forced us to lower our standards as to what constituted a "suitable" movie, but that seems unlikely since our standards were already quite low. I cannot recall a single time when we chose not to go to "the show" because there was "nothing good on." When I use the term "we" I am referring to myself and assorted neighborhood friends. Our group would number between two and six. Between the ages of seven and twelve, I saw nearly one hundred movies each year.

Theatres almost always showed "double features," so each time a person went they would see two movies. I was well into my thirteenth year before I had to buy an adult ticket. A slight bit of facial hair gave me away, and suddenly all three theatres seemed to have been alerted to my deception. Even at the Strand, the shabbiest of the trio, the ticket seller laughed when I requested a child's ticket. From that point on, a ticket cost the outrageous price of twenty-five cents.

There was one time of year that my moviegoing habit would be brought to a complete stop. That was the Lenten season. Beginning in late January, I would regularly count the number of days until Ash Wednesday and would often recount it to ensure its accuracy, all the while calculating the number of movies I would be missing because every year I "gave up" movies for Lent. Technically speaking I never willingly "gave up" movies, but I certainly stopped seeing them during that season. It would be more accurate to say that movies were given up for me, as was candy. Abstaining from candy was not much of a sacrifice, nothing in comparison to abstaining from the "silver screen."

The trauma I suffered by having to quit "cold turkey," even though I knew it was inevitable, was intensified by my less reverent friends who did not give up movies for Lent. They took pleasure in describing in great detail what I had been missing, and they would sometimes act out the most pivotal scenes. They were at their best when portraying the action of a serial, and they also enjoyed regaling me with the "Upcoming Attractions," additional movies that I would have to miss due to my reverent nature.

Even though it was painful for me, I could not resist reading the movie advertisements in the *Eagle-Star* every night. There was not a doubt in my mind that the best movies came to town during Lent. While it was true that Sis and Pat also gave up movies and candy, it was not nearly as much of a sacrifice for them. She adhered to the quaint practice of only attending movies that she expected to be good, a practice to which I never subscribed, and Pat was not at all enamored with them and rarely went. Also, he was old enough to escape detection if he chose to do so. While the forty days of atonement dragged along and I was feeling extremely sorry for myself, my father was making a sacrifice of his own. Ordinarily at the end of his workday, before walking home, he might stop at Harold's Knight Kap for a beer and a shot of whiskey. For Lent, however, he would give up all alcohol. Regardless, the sacrifices made by others, in my estimation, were insignificant. Mine were nothing short of monumental.

Albert Einstein considered it most important that a person know the location of the library. It was easy to find the library because the town was small and the Stephenson Public Library was a half block from our house. Although I do not recall the day I got my first library card it was at Mary Lou's direction, and she most likely accompanied me there. She also introduced me to the card catalog and showed me how to find books. Laura Bush, a former librarian, is reported to have said that the most valuable thing in her wallet was her library card. Considering her previous occupation, she may be biased on the subject, but I shared that sentiment for many years. During my early years, the only other card I carried in my wallet was my Clean Plate Club membership card, which I carried in case my membership in that elite organization was ever questioned. It wasn't.

The library almost became a second home for me since it was so close and the librarians were so helpful. I might go there to do my homework. Other times I would go there to read magazines, sometimes when I should have been doing homework. When it came to finding a book I could always depend on Rita Mangin to recommend one that I would invariably enjoy. When I was in sixth grade, she suggested books by Howard Pease that I still recall with pleasure. The main character in most of his books was young Tod Moran who had countless adventures while working on tramp steamers and visiting seaports all around the world. A tramp steamer is a ship that, unlike traditional cargo carriers, does not follow a fixed schedule, and carries cargo wherever it is hired to go.

Some of the books were set on the docks and waterfront streets of San Francisco, but in most of the stories Tod was a hired hand on a ship headed for trouble. Whether on land or sea he would always encounter plenty of mysteries and experience constant danger. For an upstanding young man Tod had a knack for finding jobs on disreputable ships with creepy crewmates and captains with sinister motives. Raging seas, typhoons, and shipwrecks were to be expected, but when combined with smuggling, mutiny, and even cannibals, the books were page-turners that I could not put down. Titles like *Fog Horns*, or *Secret Cargo*, or *The Ship without a Crew*, suggest trouble ahead, and readers were never disappointed. Over the years, Tod was able to work his way up from the lowest of jobs, wiper in the engine room, to first mate, but he had to overcome many obstacles along the way. Landlubber that I was I could not imagine myself in the predicaments in which Tod found himself, but I could imagine how he must have felt during his many stressful experiences. At times I wondered how someone as smart and resourceful as Tod could regularly sign on with captains who were so evil and scheming. All I could conclude was that all sea captains at that time must have been evil and scheming. Never did I allow such thoughts to interfere with my enjoyment of his stories.

Most of what we learned about the war we learned from newspapers and radio, but movies would sometimes provide additional details, some more accurate than others. A double feature would also include a three-minute newsreel, "News of the Day," which would usually focus on the war. Seeing it on the big screen made the war seem even more real. New war dramas came out at an amazing speed, and I saw every one of them (unless it was the Lenten season). Accuracy would sometimes be sacrificed for an emotional effect, but I was never a stickler for accuracy in my movies, as long as there was plenty of action. German soldiers were generally portrayed as big, loud, angry, arrogant, and not very bright. They also seemed to do a lot of snarling and grunting. Americans, on the other hand, were more tight-lipped, intelligent, determined, and humble. I assumed that these were accurate depictions until the day I saw some actual German soldiers.

It was a sunny morning in early June and I was riding my bike up and down our block, waiting for the neighborhood to come to life, when I saw an army truck stopped at our town's only traffic light. When army trucks came through town there was usually a convoy of them, and I liked to stand on the curb and wave my flag in their honor. Although I didn't have my flag that day, I raced to the corner, expecting ten or twelve trucks, but there was only one. Instead of continuing northward over the bridge into Michigan as the others had always done, this truck stopped at the Standard Oil station, right where I stood, to get gas.

The truck's canvas top had been rolled up, probably because it was a warm day, and I could clearly see the twenty men seated in the back of the truck. Instead of wearing military green uniforms, they wore tan clothing, and I was perplexed by that. Then I noticed POW printed in large black letters on the back of the shirts, and I was thunderstruck. When my heart started pounding and my eyes bulging the lone guard approached me and said, "Don't try to talk to them," and I promised that I would not. With or without that admonition I was not about to share military secrets with the enemy, even if I could have spoken German.

As soon as the truck departed, heading for Michigan, I rushed to tell my friends about my experience, and they didn't believe me. They thought that I was making the story up, especially when I described how normal the POWs looked. They scoffed when I said that the prisoners looked like everyone else in town, and nothing like the German soldiers in the movies.

Four or five more times that summer someone would see a solitary army truck carrying POWs stopped at the corner gas station, and by September all my friends had become believers. Our code word became "Germans" and whenever someone shouted it, you would see a half dozen boys furiously pedaling their bikes the half block to the corner station. We remained mystified, however, by the benign appearance of the prisoners until finally concluding that the "really tough" ones, the snarling savages from the movies, never got captured or, if they did, were being sent elsewhere. We concluded that what we were seeing were probably the leftovers.

Years later, I learned that while 7,500,000 Americans were overseas fighting in the war, our government had transported nearly 500,000 German POWs to the United States, to work in essential jobs in factories, construction, and on farms. The "leftovers" we saw were headed to northern Michigan to build an air force base. It was an exciting summer for the neighborhood kids, and we had plenty of stories to tell our classmates who did not have the good fortune to live downtown.

My father was a casual rather than rabid sports fan, but the sport in which he was most interested was boxing. After graduating from high school he had joined a local boxing club that met several nights each week, and he remained an active member for approximately five years. He never talked about wins or losses, but he derived much pleasure from the club, and he followed the sport for most of his life.

To his way of thinking, Jack Dempsey (the "Manassas Mauler") was the greatest fighter of all time, and Rocky Marciano was a distant second. He felt that Joe Louis (the "Brown Bomber"), world heavyweight champion for twelve years, was overrated as were most of the other competitors.

Professional boxing was second only to baseball in popularity from the 1930s until 1950, and even after its popularity began to wane, boxing continued to enjoy a huge fan base. My father and I would often listen to fights on our Bremer-Tully radio. I would be lying on the floor and he, sitting on a chair would be crouched over with an ear close to the speaker.

Since the nearest radio station that broadcast the fights was in Chicago, static would often make listening a challenge.

One night in autumn of 1946, when heavyweight champion, thirty-two-year-old Joe Louis, fought a relatively unknown twenty-three-year-old Tami Mauriello, it was not expected to be much of a fight. At the opening bell, when Maueriello charged across the ring and sent Louis against the ropes with a hard right hook, Dad exclaimed, "How about that!" Louis then proceeded to demolish the young challenger, knocking him out before the first round had concluded, but the excitement of such unexpected moments helped maintain the sport's popularity.

Major championship boxing matches attracted widespread attention and were discussed for days, both before and after the fight. In 1941, Joe Louis fought Billy Conn, an Irish American, who was ten pounds lighter, faster, and very clever, in a match scheduled for fifteen rounds. Conn had an impressive record and was viewed as "the great white hope." Race was never a major factor locally since in the town of 14,178 residents there was not a single African American. Nevertheless, there was eager anticipation throughout the community. Posters in store windows with pictures of the combatants advertised the event and the local radio station on which it would be broadcast, WMAM (Wisconsin Michigan Air Messenger). After twelve rounds, Conn was leading on two of the three judges' cards. In the thirteenth round, Conn disregarded his trainer's instructions and, thinking that he could score a knockout, went toe-to-toe with Louis. There was a knockout in the fourteenth round, but Billy Conn was the victim. Joe Louis retained the heavyweight title in a fight regarded as one of the best ever.

The public was excited at the prospect of a rematch, but World War II got in the way. It was not until 1946 that the rematch could be held, and again there was a big buildup. Newspaper articles from the fighters' training camps would be a daily feature, and would be widely read, stoking the public interest. The rematch, however, was a major disappointment with Louis winning by a knockout in the eighth round of a one-sided fight.

For nearly two years following my mother's death, it was Mary Lou who had held the household together. At the age of ten, she became the main grocery shopper, housekeeper, and occasional cook. She also did the laundry, but she found time to read me bedtime stories every night, made sure I said my prayers, checked my schoolwork, and gave me helpful advice. Since I had not once been asked to sing during this time I sensed that my singing career was not to be, so I needed and appreciated all the advice she offered. Pat would sometimes help out at the shop after school, and he was a font of practical advice. The summer following his sophomore year of high school Pat worked at the shop and was paid one dollar per day. Despite her many responsibilities, Mary Lou earned good grades through twelve years of school; however, my father was very set in his ways and did not believe in higher education for women.

While Mary Lou did most of the housework, there was one chore that Pat had to assist with every night: doing the dishes. They were supposed to alternate roles with the washer on one day becoming the dryer the next day and so forth, but they found something to argue about every night, and they were loud. If my dad was not at work, he would be in the living room, ear close to our Bremer Tully radio trying to listen to Gabriel Heater and the latest news of the war. Almost every night, he would have to yell, "You kids be quiet in there. I'm trying to listen to the news." On a good night, he would only yell once, but usually it was two or three times, and the news program lasted only fifteen minutes. Family life was somewhat hectic and disorganized, but we were used to it. For us it was normal, but a big change was coming.

There'll Be Some Changes Made

We had finished eating supper and were still sitting at the kitchen table when Dad informed us that he was going to get married. Although he had been a widower for nearly eighteen months, none of us, his children, had ever anticipated such a thing ever happening. My father was not one to make lengthy pronouncements, but he did say that she had been a "close friend of your mother when they were younger," and added, "It'll be good for you kids." A few days later, while the three of us were still trying to recover from that shock, he said that he and Charlotte were going to Milwaukee that weekend to get married and added, "Don't tell anyone." As soon as the three of us were alone, Pat asked Sis, "What's he going to do with her? Keep her in a deep freeze?"

Charlotte Guay was forty-three years old, from Menominee, and had never been married. She had lived with her mother, a slightly older sister, and a younger brother in a small, tidy house for her entire life. She had been employed as an assistant to the register of deeds for Menominee County for more than ten years but had just quit her job. If you were looking for a person who was well-organized, disciplined, and neat, she would be the ideal candidate. If, on the other hand, you were seeking someone warm, empathetic, and tender, you would have to continue looking.

She was used to being in charge. For example, when it was time for the older sister to enter elementary school her mother held her back a year so that they would be in the same class and she would have Char to guide her. When she was in her early twenties, Char had a friend from high school who lived in Chicago and had a new car. The two of them decided to drive out west to see the Grand Canyon and other attractions, but when Char got to Chicago, her friend had a change of heart. Although she knew how to drive, she had grown afraid of making such a long trip, so Char promised her that she would drive the entire trip, and she did. Even though she had never driven a car before.

She had been raised under especially difficult circumstances. Her mother, Ann Sullivan, was widowed twice while the children were still young. When Char was nine years old, her mother took a job cooking three meals a day at a lumber camp in northern Michigan. She would remain at the camp from late October until the middle of March because the snow made travel impossible. She kept that job for ten years, and for five months of each of those ten years Char was in charge back at home.

When Char told her mother that she was thinking of getting married, her mother said, "You'd have to be crazy to get married." It was our good fortune that she did not heed her mother's words, but years went by before we recognized that.

Our mother's death had changed our lives forever, but we had slowly and painfully adapted to that, more or less. When Dad was with us, we were always attentive to his questions, requests, or instructions, but he wasn't around that much since he was usually working. When he was absent, our lifestyle became more laid back, bordering on the slovenly.

Our mother was a tough act to follow. She had always made sure that every day was a happy one, filled with laughter and music. She was irreplaceable, and even the thought that someone would try to take her place upset all three of us. To say that Char was met with a frosty reception would have been an understatement.

Pat was resistant, angry that our mother died, and angrier still that someone came to replace her. Sis was more tolerant, and I did everything Char told me to do, but I did it grudgingly. Here was a middle-aged woman with little, if any, experience with children, finding herself in a quagmire with three resentful and suspicious children who now missed their mother more than ever. More than once she probably wished that she were back in her family home with her two docile siblings who had always done as she suggested.

From the day Char arrived we knew that she meant business. She came armed with three mantras: 1. Pick it up. 2. Put it away. 3. Keep your hands off the woodwork, and an overriding and constant message of Do It Now. For us these were new and revolutionary ideas. While we may have occasionally heard such outlandish "suggestions" before, we rarely practiced them. Now, not only did we hear them repeatedly, but we were also expected to actually do them.

Char entered into marriage with the very best of intentions, but her expectations were probably unrealistic. The first four or five years were quite tumultuous. Dad and Char argued often, always after I was in bed, but I could hear them and was scared. At least twice, Char told him that she was going home to her mother, packed a suitcase, and went home. After two days she would return, and no mention would be made of it. During her absence, Sis would be thrust into the role of cook.

My father was a frugal man, and his arguments with Char were invariably about money. He thought that she spent too much on food, and he felt that our family should be able to live on no more than one dollar a day worth of groceries. It is true that food was much cheaper at that time. A loaf of bread cost thirteen cents and a gallon of milk fifty cents. A dozen eggs sold for thirty-three cents and a pound of coffee for forty-two cents. Despite the low cost of food, however, feeding a family of four for one dollar a day was near-impossible, but she tried.

If my father had given Char more emotional support, our family's period of adjustment might have been of shorter duration, but an occasional "You listen to Char" seemed to be the extent of the support. Several times, frustrated with my inability to button my shirt correctly, she shook my shoulders slightly and exclaimed, "You are so dumb," but I didn't believe her because my teachers had been telling me the opposite. Somewhat lacking in confidence, however, I would go to Sis for a second opinion, and she would tell me, "You're the opposite of dumb, you're smart." Char was often angry and frustrated, usually for good reason, but she was not a mean person. While there was plenty of anger, there was never any abuse or violence of any sort, unless being forced to listen to the Bell Telephone Hour every Thursday night might be considered abuse. Florence, Char's sister, worked for Michigan Bell for many years and her whole family thought highly of the company. For one slow-moving hour every Thursday night, we would hear the Bell Telephone Orchestra directed by Donald Voorhees. Most of the music was classical, and, except for Char, we were not appreciative listeners.

It took a long time for us to get reasonably comfortable with Char and for her to get comfortable with us, not that we ever gave any thought to the second part of that equation. There was no shortage of arguments and disagreements, and I would sometimes present my grievances to my father although it was difficult to find him alone. My best chance to talk with him came during the five minutes he was shaving, immediately after supper and before he left for his six hours of teaching. His advice to me was almost always the same: "Listen to her, and do what she tells you to do." Although the advice did not solve any problems, it was nice to have a caring adult to whom one could whine.

The one thing that no one ever complained about was Char's cooking. The three or four ladies who had been hired to cook for us had all prepared decent meals, but it was obvious to us right from the start that Char was in a different league. She tried to adhere to Dad's one dollar "rule" by shopping for bargains, but her meals were always good, and they often came with desserts. Our palates never had it so good. She could be frugal too. If we were having cold cereal for breakfast she would cut up a small banana into slices thin enough to read a newspaper through, but all five of us would enjoy banana with our cereal.

She was also an excellent baker, and she baked a pie almost every Friday. Her cookies were special, but they came with an injunction: "Don't carry cookies or any snacks out of the kitchen. Eat them at the kitchen table. Otherwise you'll make a mess." Superman, a popular comic book hero, was reputed to have vision superior to any human. Although he possessed x-ray, heat, telescopic, and microscopic vision, he would have been no match to Char when it came to crumb detection. She could spot a crumb on the living room carpet from a distance of ten feet or more, and when she did, we would hear about it. Her sermonette usually began with, "How many times do I have to tell you?"

Char could handle a needle and thread like a tailor and made mundane tasks such as darning socks or replacing a button seem simple. She also made dresses for herself and for Mary Lou, dresses that looked like they had been purchased at the Style Shop, or some other upscale clothing store. A few days after I made a casual comment about wishing I had a chartreuse shirt she had sewn one for me, and it fit perfectly. According to a magazine that Pat brought home from his job at the news agency, chartreuse was a "hot" new color, and I felt that I made a bold fashion statement when I wore my new shirt to school, although I do not recall any comments from classmates. Neither I nor my classmates could have been considered fashion mavens, and like everything else, there was a shortage of cloth to make clothing, with the apparent exception of chartreuse-colored cloth. It was common to wear "hand-me-downs," clothing that had been worn earlier by an older relative or neighbor, and that clothing was often somewhat drab. I liked my chartreuse shirt and expected to soon see classmates sporting garments of that special color, but a trendsetter I was not. Somewhere on a shelf in the backroom of the Bell Store, a bolt of chartreuse cloth lingered virtually untouched and intact, still awaiting a swarm of frenzied customers finally recognizing the unique vibrancy of that special color.

Since she had lived through difficult times, Char was already attuned to the value of money, but her frugality probably reached new heights when she married my father. Whenever I would go to her with shoes that were already too tight, she would press down on the toe and say, "Looks like we can get another month or so with them."

My father rarely displayed a bad temper, but he could be stern, and he was no more lavish with his praise than he was with his spending. One day at supper, he said that "people around town were talking about what nice kids we have." Char responded with a noncommittal "hmm," and that was the end of that. Another time he told me that the dentist had come to the shop and told him that I was his "best patient." There were probably a few other instances in which praise was given, but those were the only memorable ones. Just as was true of commodities such as butter, sugar, and meat, positive feedback was in short supply.

The kitchen was the warmest room in the house because the stove or oven was so often in use. The other rooms would ordinarily be slightly cooler but comfortable. The one type of warmth that was lacking was the human warmth that I noticed in the houses of my friends. The only time I ever heard the word "love" used was in songs on the radio or in religion class at school.

Shortly after Dad and Char got married, she got a phone call from her former boss, the register of deeds, urging her to return to work on a part-time basis, but she declined to do so. Three years later, after several more requests, and with my father's agreement, she began working afternoons and continued for approximately ten years. Her earnings provided a cushion to the family budget, and fortunately, the meals she prepared remained as good as ever.

Unfortunately, she continued to enforce her "rules" for household management as vigorously as ever, and her scrutiny for violations continued unabated. Years later, when I was drafted into the army, I found the behaviors expected by the military no more demanding than those I had learned at home. The physical expectations were more stringent, but I managed to meet them.

There was never a doubt in my mind that the US would win the war. I had seen enough war movies to recognize that our troops were superior to those of our enemies in every regard; however, there were moments when it felt like the war would never end. Tuesday, May 8, was just another school day until the principal announced that Germany had surrendered, and cheers from all the classrooms began ricocheting off the walls of the three-story building. As a nine-year-old, another recollection of V-E (Victory in Europe) Day was that the streets were suddenly full of cars with drivers honking their horns nonstop, a cacophony unlike anything I had ever heard. Classes were not dismissed early, but most of the day was spent at the windows watching and hearing motorcade mayhem in wonderment. In other words, a great day, but nothing in comparison to V-J Day, when Japan surrendered, four months later. It was Sunday, September 2, Labor Day weekend, and it seemed like the entire population descended on Dunlap Square and blocked all traffic for the entire day. The square was jam-packed with people, dancing, singing, shouting, and snake-dancing late into the night, relieving some of the tension that built up during the forty-four months of war. Living where we did, we had a front row seat to observe the celebration, and watching adults acting crazy was a new and entertaining experience for me.

During the war, most manufacturing companies discontinued their normal production and began manufacturing war materials as directed by the government. When the war ended companies returned to domestic production, and that is when many families, including mine, purchased their first electric refrigerator. The brand was Coldspot, approximately nine cubic feet in size, and it came from Sears Roebuck. Until that time, food was kept cold in an icebox.

Our icebox was one-fourth the size of a modern refrigerator, constructed of wood and painted yellow. The inside was lined with tin, and contained a compartment big enough to hold a large block of ice. The icebox had legs three inches long, which provided space underneath for a shallow "drip pan" to catch the water from the melting ice. Woe to any child who allowed the water to overflow the pan on to the kitchen floor. We were told not to open the icebox unless it was important, instructions easily overlooked when no one was looking, and to always close the door quickly. "Don't let the ice melt!" was a familiar injunction.

Ice was available in blocks of twenty-five, fifty, or one hundred pounds, and it was delivered by a horse-drawn wagon. A fifty-pound block would cost approximately twenty cents and would last four or five days. Ice companies provided small signs to be put in a front window to indicate when more ice was needed. The iceman used heavy tongs to lift the block of ice, carry it into the house, and place it in the special compartment inside the icebox. The delivery wagons would attract kids looking for slivers of ice, and if the iceman was in a good mood he might shave off a few small pieces. Otherwise, there were often little chunks on the wagon or on the road, and those morsels were considered a real delicacy. The primary purpose of ice was to preserve food rather than for human consumption.

Most of the ice used in the twin cities came from the Menominee River. Winters were colder and lasted longer than is the case today, and by late December the ice "harvest" would have begun. Workers used ice saws and axes to cut the ice into strips, approximately ten feet long, one foot wide, and eight inches thick. With long steel picks, they slid the ice ashore and on to a conveyor belt that would move it on to a wagon, which when full would carry the ice to an icehouse. Cox's icehouse, one mile outside of town and adjacent to the river, was wooden, weather-beaten, windowless, and heavily insulated. There the ice strips would be sawed into twenty-five, fifty, or one-hundred-pound blocks, covered with sawdust for additional insulation, and stacked up. The sawdust was procured from lumber mills located along the river. It was crucial that the ice supply be sufficient to last through the months of mild weather, at least until mid-October when the basement would again be cold enough to store perishable food. The ice business was prominent and profitable for many years, and since ice was such a heavy commodity there was no such thing as a puny iceman.

Television became available in major cities several years earlier, but it arrived in Marinette in 1954, when WBAY-TV began broadcasting in Green Bay. One year later, we got our first television set. It was a Zenith floor model with a nineteen-inch screen and it was connected to an antenna on the roof. As was true of all television at that time the pictures were in black-and-white.

Now we were watching boxing matches two night per week. On Wednesday it was the Pabst Blue Ribbon Fight, and on Friday the Gillette Cavalcade of Sports from Madison Square Garden. We were seeing the biggest names in boxing as well as many less well known, some on their way up and others struggling to remain relevant, but all of them interesting. One of our favorites was a serious contender in the middleweight division, Holly Mims. Although Mims never won a championship, he was a skillful boxer and a ferocious fighter whose record was sixty-four wins and twenty-seven losses. Occasionally, you might watch a boxer who seemed to be "coasting," seeking to get a paycheck without incurring any damage, but that was never the Holly Mims approach. His pace was fast and his attack was brutal and unrelenting. By the end of any one of his fights, it would seem that a minimum of two months would be required for his recovery, but in only three or four weeks he would be back in the ring. He set the gold standard for both tenacity and resilience.

Professional wrestling was another sport that leaped into popularity with the growth of television. The three major television networks all showed live wrestling every week throughout the 1950s, and the audience for it was huge. Even though most of the public thought that the matches were fake and staged, it was considered great entertainment. In the typical match there would be a well-liked fighter pitted against one detested by the fans, a hero and a villain, and it would be difficult to turn away from the histrionics that ensued. We watched wrestling occasionally at home, but my father thought it was ridiculous, and "not a real sport." True fans, however, had their favorites, many of whom became nationally known. Among the most famous were Gorgeous George, Vern Gagne, Andre the

Giant, Hulk Hogan, and Rowdy Roddy Piper. Perhaps the United States needed a way to unwind from the bleak years of the war, and wrestling satisfied that need.

On the day that placards in store windows announced an upcoming wrestling match in town with former heavyweight champion Joe Louis as referee, my father laughed and said that Louis must be desperate for money. The day before the event, he told me that he had bought tickets for us. I was astonished since he thought highly of neither professional wrestling nor Joe Louis. The new gymnasium at Lourdes School was packed, and additional seats, surrounding the ring, had been placed on the basketball court. More than one thousand people were in attendance. There were two preliminary matches, and although none of the wrestlers were well-known, they played their roles well and the crowd enjoyed it. Immediately before the main event, Joe Louis entered the ring to loud applause. When he gave his instructions to the fighters and each time he had to separate them, there were cheers. Late in the match, he stepped in to separate the combatants again, and one of the fighters shoved him. Joe immediately went into his distinctive stance with his body at a forty-five degree angle from the troublemaker, and the crowd went wild. Everyone, including my dad, was on their feet shouting. He would sometimes comment if he felt that some item or event had not been worth the money paid for it, but he never said that about Joe Louis and the wrestling matches.

Although my father never earned much money, his accomplishments were impressive. He owned three houses, and derived rental income from all three. Our house had two apartments upstairs. The "little house," two doors down from ours, housed a single family, and the "corner house" next to the shop had two apartments' downstairs and three small apartments upstairs. While none of the houses were showplaces, all three of them were functional with low rent that attracted persons living on a limited income.

Our house was built by a wealthy lumberman at the turn of the century, probably between 1895 and 1905. Its original shape was that of a large square box. It had two floors, and was probably quite elegant when first built. The upper third of a large bay window on the front was made of stained glass as was a smaller window on the side, and there was a spacious butler's pantry next to the kitchen on the first floor. The elegance began to fade when the owner decided to build a one story attached garage in the back, and even more when a small apartment was added to one side of the garage. A later addition of a storage room to the other side of the garage did not enhance the appearance of the house. This series of "afterthoughts" eradicated whatever flowing lines that the structure once featured.

While the house was not especially solid, the additions were even less so and cold weather would remind us of that. When strong winds would howl, the walls would answer with creaks and groans, and the radiators would join in with a loud clanging sound. Radiators were cast iron devices, present in most rooms, that were connected to the furnace. Steam heat flowed from the furnace to the radiator, which could get very hot. Before going to bed I might put my underwear on the radiator to insure early morning warmth.

What had been designed to provide sumptuous lodging for a single family had been converted into an apartment house before my father purchased it, but it was probably the main reason he bought it. Upstairs in the front was a two bedroom apartment, and in the rear a small one bedroom unit with a private entrance.

Except for a tiny apartment in the back, we occupied the entire first floor. We had a large living room, dining room, and kitchen on one side of the house, and two bedrooms connected by a bathroom on the other. The living room had four windows, one of which was a large bay window. During daylight hours the room had an abundance of natural light. Above the piano hung a framed reproduction of a painting of George Washington working in his blacksmith shop at Mount Vernon. Wearing a leather apron, common to that occupation, he is using a pair of long-handled tongs to hold a piece of red-hot iron on the anvil while hammering it into the desired shape. Alongside of him is a young African American man tending to the forge. Standing much too close to the anvil and to the forge are two young children dressed in their Sunday best, a guaranteed recipe for trouble. Unless they step back from harm's way, they will get extremely dirty or, worse yet, incinerated. The painting is entitled "George Washington at the Anvil," and in small print at the bottom, "Compliments of the Phoenix Horseshoe Company."

The small apartment, adjacent to our kitchen, had been occupied by the same man for as long as I could remember. His name was Morris, and he was single. He was in his late forties, slightly too old to have been drafted into military service, and he worked as a tombstone salesman. We saw very little of him since he had a private entrance, and we heard even less, possibly because our noise drowned out whatever sounds he might have made. One day he told my father that he was moving out and getting married. That was the day that Pat and I were happy to learn that we would have our own bedroom. Until then we had shared a sofa bed in the living room.

A week later Morris moved out, the long-locked kitchen door was opened, and our living space expanded. The bedroom was fairly spacious, plus, there was a small bathroom attached, a big step up for us. We had always heard that this room had been an "afterthought" of the original owner, but did not recognize the significance of that designation until the advent of cold weather. Very little heat made it back to this room, and we would sleep under a mound of blankets. When it was bitter cold outside the water in the toilet bowl would freeze as would the water lines to our sink, but we managed to adapt to such conditions. One night at approximately 2:00 a.m., Pat and I were awakened by soft knocking on the door of our private entrance. Pat answered the door, and a woman was surprised to learn that Morris no longer lived there. When Pat returned to bed, I asked him what he thought a woman would want in the middle of the night. His chuckle told me that he knew something that I did not know, but all he said was "Go back to sleep."

The basement was the nerve center of the house. It had a floor and foundation of poured concrete, and a furnace and stoker stood in the middle of it. Off to the side there was a coal bin, a small room in which coal was stored. The coal bin had a hinged metal door in the concrete foundation, and coal would be delivered by a dump truck through the coal door into the bin. When we knew the coalman was coming we would have to remember to unlatch the metal door and prop it open slightly so that the coalman could do his job without having to enter the house. The coalman would always be covered with coal dust, and even we kids recognized that his entry would do little for household cleanliness.

Keeping the house warm required considerable effort. Each day during the heating season someone would fill the stoker with approximately twenty shovels full of coal, carried in a coal shovel the twenty or twenty-five feet from the bin. The stoker would automatically feed coal into the furnace as directed by the thermostat upstairs. The stoker was often called the "hopper," as in "Go fill the hopper." Filling the hopper was not backbreaking labor, but did require some effort since it stood four feet high and was loaded from the top. Every night long-handled tongs would be used to extract the "clinker," the remains of the burned coal from the furnace. The clinker would usually be circular in shape with a diameter of twenty-four inches, identical to the grate inside the furnace, and the same size as the front door of the furnace. Whenever I was able to remove the clinker intact I felt victorious, however, that did not happen often. Usually I had to remove it in two or three pieces. The red-hot clinker would then be deposited into a bushel basket made of corrugated metal. The baskets had rope handles and had to be carried up to the curb for the twice-weekly trash pickup. The heating system at the corner house was identical to the system at our house, and our daily duties were identical at both houses. Many of the houses in town were heated by coal at that time. Coal was ordered by the ton, and coal trucks were a very familiar sight.

The ceiling of the basement was high enough to allow an adult to stand upright, except where the presence of heating ducts prevented it. Almost every room in the house had a radiator, and each radiator was connected to a duct. The ducts resembled the tentacles of an octopus except the ducts were much thicker and were wrapped in an asbestos fabric. The purpose of the fabric was to insulate the ducts and prevent heat loss. An unintended benefit was the cushion it provided when I bumped my head on it as I often did. The labyrinth of ducts overhead created a sense of confinement that reminded me of the interior of a submarine, based on the war movies I had seen, and I would sometimes pretend that I was in a submarine. There was a window at sidewalk level in the front of the basement, and that would be my periscope. The feet of people walking by were the Nazi U-boats that were then wreaking havoc on US troop transport ships in the North Atlantic, and I would fire torpedoes at them. It did not matter if the U-boats were oxfords, saddle shoes, or galoshes, my aim was deadly, and I sunk every one of them.

When my father announced that he was running for sheriff of Marinette County, I was dumbfounded, since my perception of a sheriff was based on what I had seen in the movies. How could a person who never owned a horse, a six-shooter, nor a cowboy hat, serve as a sheriff, I asked

JAMES LAHIFF

myself. Local politics was a frequent topic of conversations at the shop, and many people, my father included, felt that there was room for improvement in the way the current sheriff performed his duties.

He was one of six candidates on the Republican ticket in the primary election, and he ran on a theme of "Able, Honest, and Energetic" (see last page), adjectives that aptly described him. Had I been asked I would have included "dependable" since he was a person who always did what he said he would do. Because he felt that his work was more important than campaigning, he did not campaign much, and consequently he did not win the election. Being sheriff is a full-time job, and it seems unlikely that he would have been able to close the shop for the two-year term had he been elected. The prospect of having a father who was a sheriff had lost some luster the day I learned that family members did not also get to wear badges.

Don't Stop Thinking About Tomorrow

Ever since I entered first grade religion had been an important part of the curriculum, and it was on a Monday in third grade that we were introduced to the Baltimore catechism. One segment of it was presented in a question/answer format, and we were told that we would each be given an oral exam on that segment within the next three weeks. We had to learn the answers to a list of twenty-five questions, stand in front of the class, and be grilled by Sister Angela. When several of the scholars groaned at the thought of such an ordeal, she offered an option. Instead of having to respond to all the questions at one time we could answer the questions in bunches, five one day, five another, as long as we learned (i.e., memorized) all twenty-five within the three-week period. That seemed doable, if not especially appealing.

When I showed Sis the material that I had to learn and described the oral quiz that was required, she said that it would be easy for me to accomplish it in much less than three weeks. We got to work on it immediately and on Thursday night of the first week, she proclaimed me ready to answer all the questions the next day. I balked at that and she agreed that I could wait until Monday. She always had more confidence in me than I had in myself. Over the weekend, we devoted a few more hours to the questions until I felt fully prepared.

At the start of religion class on Monday, Sister asked if there was anyone who "would like" to answer some of their questions. If truth be told, the number of students who would actually "like" to do that would be zero. Simply put, we were doing this because we had to do it, but this did not seem the right time to make that distinction. Three students raised their hands to answer questions, but I did not because I was still not sure. Each of the first two kids answered five questions, and the third answered three. Sister told the first two that they were making good progress and reminded the third that five was the minimum number allowed.

I had been pondering whether I might put it off for one more day, but the prospect of testing my sister's good nature motivated me to tentatively raise my hand when Sister asked if there were any more volunteers. "Well, Jimmy, how many questions do you think you can handle?" she asked. When I responded "All of them," a boy behind me shouted, "What?" and there was loud murmuring throughout the class. I walked to the front of the classroom and breezed through the twenty-five questions, starting with "Who is God?" (the Supreme Being who made all things) to "Why were you born?" (to know, love, and serve God) and all points in between.

When I finished, Sister simply said "Fine," and the class moved along to other things. Having expected a few more accolades for my accomplishment, I was puzzled by her terse response as well as the chill that had come over the class. At recess one classmate called me a "showoff," another asked me why I had to be such a "teacher's pet" and a third threatened to punch me in the nose, three clear indicators that my performance had not been well received. This was my introduction to the negative aspects of being a rate buster. That was a learning experience for me, but, apparently, I had completely forgotten it when I was confronted with a similar situation nine years later.

Then I was seventeen years old and had just graduated from high school and had gotten a summer job at a factory that made wooden boxes. The company had a quota system that specified the productivity expected of each employee each day. Most of the plant workers operated electric saws of varying sizes, and my job required me to operate one of the smaller saws. It was my first day on the job, and when the whistle signaled lunchtime, I was feeling pretty good about myself. I followed my coworkers outdoors to a grassy area on the bank of the Menominee River, immediately adjacent to the plant. Everyone sat on the ground, opened their brown paper bags, and proceeded to eat. Afterward most of them either smoked or took a nap, since the break was an hour long. Employee cafeterias or lunchrooms were uncommon at that time, and nonexistent at the box factory.

The group was comprised of thirty men, mostly in their late forties or fifties, and I was the only new employee, therefore, a person of some curiosity, if not interest. When one of the older men asked me how it was going, I said, "Great. It's only noon and I've already beat my quota." A few snickered at that, and one man advised me not to work so hard because it was not worth it. Another added, "Work hard and you'll tire yourself out. Sometimes tired people slip and fall into the river, and it's real cold and plenty deep." I got the message that day and for the rest of the summer I reached my quota every day, but barely, and I never fell into the river.

With food and other essentials rationed, many families planted "victory gardens" to supplement their food supply. We did not have a garden, only a small patch of rhubarb, which returned each year, despite a complete lack of attention being paid to it. My father decided that raising chickens would be a good way to help meet our nutritional needs, and he and Pat built a chicken coop alongside the blacksmith shop. Before long, there were two dozen baby chicks in a large, low cardboard box with a heat lamp attached on our kitchen floor. A week later, the chicks, already somewhat larger, were taken to their new home. Pat and Sis took turns feeding them and cleaning the coop, and seemed to enjoy it, at least until the novelty wore off, approximately one month later. By then they had named each chicken and maintained that each had a distinct "chickenality." A few months later, we began getting a few eggs, and before long we were occasionally having a chicken for Sunday dinner, not as a guest but as the entrée.

After approximately one year, my father decided to discontinue the chicken project, and we were neither surprised nor displeased. There was more to raising chickens than we had anticipated. Twice a predator, probably a weasel, burrowed under the fence, and each time it killed two chickens and left the rest traumatized. Despite the fact that there had been many witnesses to the assault, none would testify, probably because they were too chicken.

Since Pat had spent the most time with the chickens he knew them better than anyone else, and he always had something to say when we sat down to enjoy one at dinner. Sometimes his remark would be no more than, "Goodbye, Elmer." Other times something longer like, "You could be feisty, Phyllis, but I enjoyed knowing you." Regardless, his remarks did not enhance the ambiance of the occasion, and we were relieved when the flock had been eliminated and the coop torn down.

One morning in late April, I was startled to find the music teacher waiting for me as I came through the front door. I had never spoken to her before, but she knew my name and she had a plan. She thought that I "might like" to sing a song at the Parent Appreciation program to be held in three weeks, and that Mary Lou "might like" to accompany me on the piano. Her "request" caught me by complete surprise since I had not been asked to sing in the past two years and had assumed that my singing career was a thing of the past. Also, my repertoire was badly outdated. Did I express any of my reasons for not wanting to sing? No, all I said was "OK."

This would be my first performance on an actual stage, but Mary Lou was already a veteran since she had participated in several piano recitals on that stage. Her most recent experience, however, had been a traumatic one. Six weeks earlier the weather was unseasonably mild and because the auditorium was stuffy, and nothing "up there" was air-conditioned the janitor had opened the doors on either side of the stage. Her playing had been flawless until she came to the most complex part of the semiclassical piece and a strong wind swept her sheet music off the piano. She struggled through the rest of the selection and vowed not to let that happen again. From that day forward, she would glue the sheet music to a piece of cardboard heavy enough to withstand the strongest wind.

I need not have worried about having to find a song to sing because the sisters had found the "perfect" song. As I recall the song was entitled "That Wonderful Daddy of Mine" and the opening line, "There's no one in the world like my daddy" conveys the main theme of the song. It was beyond melancholy. It was a warm and well-deserved tribute to my father as well as a real tearjerker. The sisters could "milk" an emotional moment with the best of them.

We devoted considerable time to practicing, both with the music teacher and at home, and the performance went well. Since Sis was occupied playing the piano while keeping the sheet music from blowing away and I was intently watching her for cues, neither of us were able to look out at the audience. Afterward, we heard that many of the ladies in the audience were dabbing their eyes. My father was present that night, but

I do not recall that he commented on it. He may not have been listening since he always had a lot on his mind, and that would have been just as well. He would have been embarrassed.

When my third-grade class was introduced to the idea of a "permanent record." it did not make much of an impression since we had already gotten used to being observed and graded. Little did we realize that it would be mentioned many times during our years at school, and that it would acquire ominous overtones. When I first started thinking about permanent records, I imagined large rooms with individuals, perhaps apprentice nuns, hunched over long tables and recording in big books how each student had performed that day. By grades six or seven, any admonishment for misbehavior might be accompanied by a veiled threat such as, "You wouldn't want that to go in your permanent record." In high school, a grim picture would be painted of the sorry individual with multiple red marks on their permanent record. "Who would want to employ that person?" We were asked to ponder it and ponder it I did. The ability to ponder has always been one of my strengths.

The fact that the subject of permanent record was only mentioned when it was related to misbehavior made it seem biased against many students. When someone would be congratulated for having won an award or for having written an outstanding book report, there was never a mention of how the accomplishment would improve his or her permanent record. The permanent record suddenly seemed like nothing but a warehouse of negative information, similar to a police blotter. Apparently, the only way that the record would show that a person had actually lived would be if there had been misbehavior. The student who never misbehaved would be out of luck. Generations of students have pondered the mystery of the permanent record, and the pondering is unlikely to cease any time soon.

Almost every winter included at least one severe storm that would curtail most normal activities, except for school and the shop. Children went to school and my father went to his shop regardless of the weather. A storm rolled in one afternoon in late January, but Pat had already decided that the weather would not keep him from driving to a Golden Gloves boxing tournament in Escanaba that night. He did not mention his plan to the family, probably because he was not allowed to drive the car, and possibly because he did yet have a driver's license. He left the house at 6:30

supposedly headed for the armory, two blocks away, to play basketball, but instead went to our garage in the back of our house where two of his friends waited for him. They quietly opened the garage doors and pushed the car onto the road and far enough away from the house for the motor to be started without being heard, and headed for Escanaba, Michigan, fifty miles to the north.

While the boys were heading north, my father was listening to the news with its frequent warnings to stay off the roads unless absolutely necessary. Pat expected to complete this escapade without being discovered because he knew that Dad would never drive on such a night. What he never could have anticipated, however, was Dad going to the garage to retrieve a cigar from the car. It was approximately 8:30 when Dad made his discovery, and that was probably when his worrying cranked up into overdrive. He may have told Char, but I went to bed unaware of the crisis, although I noticed that he was staying up later than usual and listening to the radio with the intensity usually reserved for news from the battlefront. As I dozed off, I could hear the announcer talking about sheets of ice and drifting snow caused by the gale-force winds. It was close to midnight when I was awakened by the sound of my father's quiet but stern sounding voice. Since he would occasionally talk in his sleep, and because his voice was the only one I heard, I attributed it to that.

On an ordinary day, my father was unlikely to ever raise his voice, especially not at breakfast, but this was not an ordinary day. His tirade at Pat was loud and long. I still did not know what Pat had done, but I assumed that he had committed the crime of the century. The recipe for Dad's ranting seemed to consist of two main ingredients: five tablespoons of anger at Pat for what he had done, and one teaspoon of relief that there had been no accident. There may have also been a smidgeon of admiration of Pat's resourcefulness, but that remained unspoken. I had never seen my father so angry. "From now on you're going to buckle down with your schoolwork," and "No more staying out late," were themes that had been visited before. He also told Pat that he would never drive that car again because, "Kids shouldn't be out driving cars." Since we had already been informed more than once to never expect to drive the family car, that pronouncement was about as surprising as our meal plan for Friday. Because he was in no position to mount any defense, Pat simply shrugged his shoulders and said that they had seen "some really good fights last night." After a few days family life returned to normal. Many times, I have wished that I could be easygoing like Pat instead of the rule follower that I was.

Reading was emphasized at every grade level throughout the year, but in the month of March, it was given special attention. When I was in sixth grade the theme was "Choose Books Wisely," and one day Sister Barbara told Fred, Dick, and I to see her after class. Whenever a teacher tells a student to see her after class, it is rarely to convey good news, and this was no exception. She told us that we had been "selected" to participate in a skit intended to stress the importance of reading good literature and avoiding "trash." The skit would last about ten minutes and would be presented before all twelve grades at an assembly in the auditorium.

The assembly was to be held in two weeks, and the three of us practiced in our classroom each day after class under the direction of Sister Barbara. The plot of the skit was not overly complex. For the first five minutes, the other two boys would be on stage discussing the good books they were reading and extolling the virtues of great literature. When Fred said, "There is nothing like a good book," that was my cue to come running on to the stage completely disheveled, a real mess. My white shirt would be flapping outside of my dark trousers, and my bright green sweater would be only half on. My hair would be mussed up, and I would be breathlessly describing the terrible nightmares I had been having and how I would toss around in bed, unable to get a good night's sleep. Fred and Dick would then ask me a few incisive questions about my reading habits and quickly identify comic books, filled with crime and violence, as the cause of my sleep deprivation. I would thank them for their insights and vow to change my ways. No more "trash" for me, only good books. Not exactly great drama, but it does make a point, especially if it is presented properly.

The big day arrived. Since the assembly was scheduled for the final hour of the school day, there was plenty of time to worry about the upcoming challenge in front of the entire school. When the principal finally introduced the skit she said, "This little play has an important message. Pay attention." The curtain opened and Fred and Dick launched into their scripted conversation about the importance of good books. I stood in the wings, spellbound by the floodlight shining down on to the stage, and by the thought that all twelve grades were in the audience. Suddenly, I heard my cue and charged onto the stage, hair combed, shirt and sweater perfectly in place, looking like I had just stepped out of *Gentleman's Quarterly* magazine. Fred and Dick were startled to see my neat appearance, but I emoted as best I could. We remembered our lines, but the skit lacked its intended impact. It is unlikely that any reading habits were changed that day. Later, back in the classroom, Sister congratulated us on our good job and with a smile said, "Jim, you seemed very well put together for a boy who had been experiencing such terrible nightmares."

When I got home from school that day I was feeling disappointed over the way I had messed up my role of a messed up student, especially after having rehearsed it for two weeks. Sis assured me that only two students in the whole school were aware of my mistake, and that she would not tell anyone. I consoled myself by delving into my preferred literature: comic books. "Crime Does Not Pay" and "Dick Tracy" were my favorites. I was particularly intrigued by the wrist radio that Dick Tracy always wore.

Sometime after dark in late March, when it began to seem that winter would never end, intrepid fishermen on the interstate bridge would make the first sighting of a few of the silvery fish. By noon the next day, the word would have spread, and the "smelt carnival" would begin. Smelt were bright silver fish, five or six inches long, and the smelt "run" would last for approximately ten nights as the fish swam upstream to spawn. During that time, hundreds of people would come to the interstate bridge to watch fishermen lower small nets into the water and bring up dozens of smelt at a time. The mass of fish would be so thick that the river would shine as bright as a silver bowl on a dining room table. Swarms of people, some from as far away as Chicago, would come to experience the delirium. Food vendors would be selling hamburgers and frankfurters and, in anticipation of the event, a Smelt Queen would have been elected to reign. Local eccentrics would entertain the crowd by offering to swallow a live smelt for a few coins. When fried or baked, smelt had a nice flavor, and there would be businessmen eager to buy them in large quantities. Then, with little advance warning, the night would come when there were no more smelt, and the populace would resume their yearning for an early spring.

It was mid-March when Pat and some of his buddies, all high school juniors, devised a plan to capture the smelt market by building a raft and using a large net to catch the fish in their approach to the bridge. Using wooden planks, they constructed a sturdy craft, approximately 8 feet by 8 feet, with an opening in the center that was four feet square. A pulley was attached to an overhead frame that was strong enough to support the netfuls that they anticipated, and my father welded a frame to which the net would be attached. The crew found four empty oil barrels that they attached for flotation, and they christened the raft the River Master. While waiting for the main attractions to make their appearance, one of the crew, always somewhat of a show-off, would entertain the people on the bridge by walking a narrow plank from the raft to the shore. After a few more days of waiting, he added a blindfold to his act and would walk the plank blindfolded. He would pretend to be about to fall off, and the appreciative crowd would gasp, only to applaud when he stepped onto the land. His antics turned out to be the most exciting event in a year that there was no smelt run.

When he was a senior in high school Pat got a part-time job as a custodian at the Knights of Columbus Hall. Wedding receptions and dances were often held there on Saturdays, and Pat's job was to clean it on Sunday so that it was ready for the Knights' meeting on Monday night. Ordinarily there would be a partially full keg of beer remaining from Saturday's festivities, and that would motivate the club members to attend the meeting. After three or four consecutive dry Mondays, the members decided that Pat was not "the right person" for that job.

Pat was a member of the class of '48, a group with a reputation for being high-spirited and a challenge to control. One February day in their junior year, the sister announced that she would have to leave the room for a few minutes, assigned the class several pages to read, and strongly implied that there would be a pop quiz when she returned. She said that Celeste, a top student, would be in charge and she should make notes of any misbehavior. By the time Celeste had reluctantly moved to the main desk facing the class, a boy strode to the front of the room and proceeded to give a brief but fiery speech on the subject of manhood. He concluded with a challenge: "If you are a man, you will follow me; if you are a mouse, you will stay behind." He then walked to a window, opened it, climbed on to the ledge, and jumped from the second floor down into two or three feet of snow on the ground; the other ten boys in the class did the same thing. The faculty was especially pleased when that class graduated.

Although my class never reached the pinnacle of group misbehavior attained by the class of '48, there were moments that are still etched in memory. Earl was a clever and adventurous boy who hated being cooped up in school, and one day he decided that he deserved a break in the routine. He got up from his seat in the back of the second-floor classroom, walked to a window, opened it, and stepped onto the concrete ledge that bordered the front of the school. The teacher, mentally sharp but elderly, was startled to see him on the outside looking in through the window which she opened and said, "Stop this foolishness immediately," but he had already scampered to another window. The classroom had three pairs of windows that were separated by several feet of plain brick wall. For the next few minutes, they seemed to be playing hide-and-seek with Earl, always a step or two ahead of the teacher who was unable to keep up the pace. The class watched with quiet astonishment. They were regularly entertained by Earl's penchant for playfulness, but this raised distraction to a new level, one that would never be reached again. It was not clear if he eventually rejoined the class in response to the teacher's threats or because he realized that this escapade would not enhance his permanent record, but he then left the room and walked down to the principal's office. He was quite familiar with the disciplinary process.

While paging through a *Popular Mechanics* magazine at the library one day, I saw a small advertisement for Tiny Tone crystal sets, devices that allowed a person to listen to local radio stations without an actual radio. I recognized that that was what my life had been missing, and was somehow able to scrounge up $2.99 and order one from a company in Kearney, Nebraska. It was the size of a pack of cigarettes, bright red, and made of sturdy cardboard. It had a small dial on the front and two wires, a ground and an antenna coming out the back. Each wire had a small alligator clip attached, and when I fastened the clips to the bedspring, just as advertised, I heard the radio station. The advertisement indicated that the crystal set would allow its owner to hear all local radio stations, and that proved to be true, although our town only had one station. The fact that the station was barely a block from our house made for an easy test of the set's power of reception. It was fun to lay in bed, crystal set pressed against my ear, listening to popular records and occasional comments from the announcer while everyone thought I was asleep, but the station stopped broadcasting at midnight. Some nights I would doze off in the middle of the program only to be reawakened by a loud brass band playing the national anthem, which was the customary sign off for the day. After a few months, however, bored with the routine, I concluded that what I needed was an actual radio.

At this same time, I was reading a book entitled *Strikeout Story* by Bob Feller. When he graduated from high school at age seventeen, he went directly to the major leagues, never having played in a minor league. He set many records during his long career, even though it had been interrupted by two years of service in the navy during the war. Often called "The Heater from Van Meter" (Iowa), he was the first pitcher whose fastball exceeded one hundred miles per hour, and the only one to ever throw a no-hitter on opening day. The book impressed me so much that I became a lifelong fan of the Indians, and I developed an appreciation for the city of Cleveland, Ohio. Prior to reading the book, I would have had a hard time locating Cleveland on a map of Ohio.

Baseball was called "America's Pastime" because it was the most popular sport, and it was played at many different levels. The annual baseball All-Star game was sponsored by the Chicago Tribune, and it attracted nationwide attention. The all-stars were chosen by the fans who completed ballots, which they mailed to the newspaper. Beginning several weeks before the game, each day the "Trib" would publish, on the front page of the sport section, the current vote totals for the four top vote-getters at every position. I would scour the numbers carefully, trying to estimate the likelihood that an Indian might be elected to the team. On my ballot, I voted for an Indian at every position, and I voted twice for two consecutive years, trying to tip the balance. Whenever an Indian was elected, it felt like a personal victory. Despite my attempts to stuff the ballot box, however, the New York Yankees, our archrival, would usually place twice as many players on the team as would the Indians.

After several weeks, my whining about my need for a radio paid off. Char found one in her mother's basement and gave it to me. The cabinet was made of dark brown plastic, and it had a sizeable crack in it, but it worked. It was manufactured by the Philco Company, and it had a wire attached that served as an antenna that could be attached to a bedpost or, better yet, extended outdoors through a window for improved reception. No longer shackled to a single station I was soon enjoying radio programs from Green Bay, Milwaukee, and even Chicago. There would often be static that would make listening more difficult, but my horizons were expanding and I was feeling quite cosmopolitan.

I had been immersed in late night radio for approximately two weeks before I "struck gold." That was the night that I stumbled upon WTAM, a 50,000- watt clear channel station broadcasting from Cleveland, Ohio. The announcer's name was Joe Mulvihill, and the program was sponsored by Robert Hall, a popular line of clothing. It advertised with a catchy jingle: "When the values go up, up, up/And the prices go down, down, down/Robert Hall this season/Will show you the reason/Low overheads, Low overheads." Mr. Mulvihill seemed to know everything about Cleveland and quite a bit about the Indians, even though it was not a sports program. He described the activities on Euclid Avenue so vividly that you almost felt as though you were there.

I shared the bed with Pat, who being six years older than me, came to bed later, but I often was still listening to the radio. He was baffled by my fascination with Cleveland. "Why do you care about that?" he would ask, and that was similar to the reaction I would get from friends and classmates when I tried to educate them about the wonders of that magnificent city. I remained a faithful listener for more than a year and then became more sporadic. Thanks to Joe Mulvihill, however, I continued to recognize Cleveland as one of the greatest cities in the nation, if not in the world.

My introduction to the world of business came when I became a "courier" of sorts. At the end of each month, Dad would bring his old, weather-beaten ledger home from the shop and become a bookkeeper for one evening. He would use his old (and heavy) Underwood typewriter to prepare the bills to be sent to people who owed him money, and he would write out checks to pay the bills that we owed. (See last page.) It would be my job to deliver most of the checks. Until now, I had been living large on my weekly allowance of twenty-five cents while watching Pat and Sis do most of the household chores. At that time, a postage stamp cost three cents, but money was scarce, and it was a chance for me to make myself useful.

Within the first few days of each month, I was to hand-carry checks for the various services that the family had used in the previous month. Before my first venture out to make my contribution to society I was given two instructions: watch out for cars, and always get a receipt. With the exception of an occasional check to be delivered to a store, most of my deliveries would pay for utilities.

In a small town, one might expect utility offices to be located close together but that was not the case. They were spread far enough apart that it would take me more than an hour to complete the circuit, but I enjoyed having this responsibility. I had walked or ridden past these buildings many times without giving any thought to what transpired inside, and I was excited at the prospect of being able to find out.

The water department proved to be the biggest mystery to me. It was located in a small redbrick building that resembled a fortress with windows too high for a passing pedestrian to look into. In the three years that I went there, I never saw another customer, not even one. Three middle-aged ladies worked behind desks, and it felt as though they played a game of "chicken" with the loser being the one who eventually stepped up to the counter. Whenever I walked into that office, I felt like I was interrupting something that was much more important or more fascinating than I was. I could not imagine what that might be.

The gas company was in the middle of a block of small stores, and like those stores, it was at street level and had large glass windows. When you went in to pay a bill, you would walk up to the first desk, and a lady would handle the transaction. Her desk was usually messy, and she often could not find her receipt book. "Where did that darn thing go?" she would ask me and anyone else within earshot, and I was never any help. She would then say, "It's got to be here." Once after she asked where "that darn thing" was, I volunteered, "It's got to be here," and was rewarded with a scowl. That was the day I became a mute customer. She knew that I was not the kind of person willing to leave without a receipt, however, and she would eventually find it. Since I usually paid the bills in late afternoon, I assumed that the messy desk was evidence of a hard day's work. Once or twice, however, during the summer, I went there when they opened and saw that her desk at the beginning of the day was no different from at the end of the day, a case of permanent disarray.

Whenever I went to pay the electric bill there would be two or three people ahead of me, but the line always moved quickly because it was such an efficient operation. I would hand the lady the check along with the bill, and she would give them a quick glance. Then with a flourish, she would stamp "Paid" on the bill in purple ink, hand the bill back to me, and I'd be on my way. The stamped bill would be my receipt. The whole transaction would take less than a minute. The electric company was a half block from my house and was next to the interstate bridge that crosses over the Menominee River, the boundary between Wisconsin and Michigan.

Another of my monthly stops was at the coal company. It provided the coal we used for heating our house and the other two houses that my father owned. (Property was very inexpensive in town at that time.) Since none of the houses were well insulated and winters were long and cold, we burned as much as sixty tons of coal each year. We made payments on coal every month of the year, and I was always waited on by the same man. He wore a white shirt with a bright necktie, and he was good-natured, almost boisterous. He would say, "Good day, what can I do for you?" I would mumble, "I want to pay a bill," and he'd ask, "Would you like a receipt?" I would nod, and he would say, "We'll see you next month," as I departed. We followed that same script for three years.

The telephone company was my favorite place to do business. Housed in a one-story brick building and two blocks away from downtown, it was one of the more modern buildings in town. Inside, the office walls always appeared freshly painted and the office equipment polished to a shine, as were the three young ladies who worked near the front counter. Not only were they better dressed than the other clerks with whom I dealt, they actually seemed happy to see me. One would ask, "How are you today?" and I would croak out "Fine." Another might ask what I learned in school that day, and I'd respond, "Not much," and they would laugh appreciatively at my great wit. These conversations would last no more than two or three minutes, but when I left the telephone office, I would have a spring in my step.

My next stop after the telephone company would be the post office since it was nearby, and because I considered it my civic duty to familiarize myself with the latest WANTED posters provided by the FBI. There would be six or eight posters stapled to a bulletin board with a photo of each criminal and a brief description of the crime of which that person had been charged. Typical offenses would be bank robbery, mail fraud, forgery, burglary, or, occasionally, murder, and I would stare intently at their faces. It would be a rare day if I did not feel sure that I had seen at least one of them within the last few days. One week it would be the forger that I remembered seeing in the canned goods aisle at the A&P. Another time I would distinctly recall the burglar looking at the magazines at Lundgren's Drug Store. At the bottom of each poster would be this message: "Please cause his immediate arrest and notify the authorities." I was never exactly certain how I would "cause" the criminal's arrest, but the notification part was clear, and I intended to remain vigilant.

Carrying the checks to the five business places rather than mailing them saved the family fifteen cents in postage and a few more cents in unused envelopes each month. Most valuable to me, however, were the memories I collected from my monthly excursions into the "real world," and I never considered my courier duties a chore.

Sum Sum Summertime

From the first day of September until the last day of April the days, weeks, and months advanced at a steady rate of speed. That regularity would come to an abrupt halt on the first day of May, which in most respects is a wonderful month. At last, there is a hint of summer and the aroma of lilac blossoms fills the air. While a snowfall in May is not unheard of, it is exceptional, and when it occurs, the snow melts in a day or two. The big downside of May is how the passage of time slows down. A day in May is longer than a day in any other month. Ask any grade school student. The normal six-hour school day now seems at least eight hours long, and certain classes, especially arithmetic, become unending. In late April, summer vacation seemed imminent. In mid-May, it felt like it was nothing but a rumor.

    The first two or three weeks of vacation would be as great as expected. I would be out of the house by 9:00 a.m. and back home only for meals. We would play baseball in the alley and football in a small field one block away. We would sometimes take a break and play dummy school on a staircase of twenty stairs attached to the back of an apartment building across the street where friends lived. There were several small wooded areas nearby and we would play war games and build forts there. Our daytime activities were usually only for boys. In the evening after supper, there would be a group of six or more boys and girls playing spirited games of kick-the-can, and those games would last until the first parent yelled for their child to come home. After a few weeks, however, the dullness of summer in a small town with few organized activities would set in.

That dullness would linger until you spotted the first placard in a store window advertising a circus or carnival that was coming to town. I preferred a carnival to a circus because a carnival would remain in town for a week while a circus usually stayed for only a day or two. Whether carnival or circus, it would be one of the highlights of the summer, and excitement would mount until it arrived. These were a very big deal at that time. My friends and I would ride our bikes over to the designated field weeks in advance to see if part of the show might have arrived early but, alas, that never happened.

The first carnival I can remember is one that was practically in our backyard. For the first five years of my life, there was a large field directly behind our house, and each summer for one week a big carnival would set up there with rides, games, and shows. The backs of their tents would be lined up along the backyards of our block. Pat and his friend Billy, who lived two doors away from us, always looked forward to the excitement of carnival week, and they spent considerable time on the midway. One night a policeman came to Billy's house with a complaint from several female performers who claimed that there was a man standing on a stepladder and looking down through a second floor window of their house into the ladies' dressing room which had high walls but no roof. Billy's mother said that was impossible since they didn't even own a stepladder, but she allowed the officer to come in and investigate. He walked upstairs, quietly turned the doorknob, and found Billy standing on a desk gazing down into the dressing room with binoculars. That was reported to be the one and only time that Billy had ever used his desk.

That was also the last time the field would be used for entertainment because the land was purchased by an automobile dealership. Within a year, the field we had enjoyed all year long had been transformed into a large asphalt slab littered with new Chevrolets awaiting purchase. If that weren't bad enough, it marked the last year that circuses and carnivals would operate in Marinette. The new site was a field adjacent to the Menominee airport. It was two miles away, not as convenient as the backyard, but life in pursuit of culture is rarely easy. I was confident that I would be regular in attendance at that new site next year.

By midwinter my friend Larry, who lived across the street, and I had planned our strategy for getting to the tent shows in the future. To get to a carnival his father would drive us over on Tuesday night and take us home two hours later. My father would do the same on Thursday night, and on Saturday afternoon, we would make the trip by bikes. Every aficionado of carnivals knows that for maximum enjoyment, at least three visits are required.

Our plan worked for the next three or four years, and both fathers, while not enthusiastic, did their duty. My father harbored a low opinion of such enterprises because he felt that they took too much money out of town, but he never expressed those sentiments while chauffeuring us there and back, not that it would have lessened our excitement.

On Tuesday and Thursday evenings, it was fun to walk along the midway and savor the sounds, smells, bright lights, and the crowds of people. We might ride on the Ferris wheel, bumper cars, or electric swings, and perhaps play one or two games of chance, none of which I ever won. While we may have appeared to be typical kids enjoying the ambiance, we were actually on a reconnaissance mission in anticipation of the ultimate challenge we would face on Saturday.

It was a carnival tradition that on Saturday, the gates would open at noon and all prices were greatly reduced until 6:00 p.m. No matter what weather conditions prevailed, we would be close to the front of the unruly mob, and the place would be swarming with young bargain hunters with sharp elbows. To our way of thinking, the more rides we rode and shows we saw, the more money we saved. It was simple economics.

Once through the gate our first stop would be at a food wagon because we knew that without proper nourishment we would fade long before late afternoon. With good nutrition in mind, we would have one or two hot dogs for protein and popcorn as a vegetable. Next, a cup of Pepsi for hydration followed by some cotton candy for dessert. Then we would head for the rides.

We would ride every ride on the midway, except for the kiddie rides of course, and some of them we would ride multiple times. There was one ride, however, that we always saved for Saturday. It was more challenging than any of the others, and we tested ourselves on it only once each season. It was the Tilt-a-Whirl, and we considered it the ultimate challenge. Two to four riders would be strapped onto cushioned seats with back support provided by a clam shell-like cover that partially enclosed them. The ride held six of these clams, each spinning on its own axis. The speed of the spin was determined by the weight distribution of the passengers. Who would not want to make it spin as fast as possible? The clams were attached to a flexible platform that undulated while rapidly moving in a circle. The undulation created a sensation of experiencing strong waves in a boat. The challenge was to avoid upchucking the food you had recently enjoyed. When the ride ended and the attendant unstrapped us, I would stand up on rubbery legs, take a few steps, mistakenly think that my stomach had won the battle and then end up running to the tall grass surrounding the midway, and I would not be alone. Another challenge unmet. At 6:00, we would head home on our bikes, talking about all the fun it was and vowing that next year we would beat the mechanical monster. We never did.

It was early June, I was ten years old, and I was stunned by the sign I saw in the drugstore's window. While the wild beasts, clowns, and "death defying trapeze artists" that were illustrated in bright reds, yellows, and blues were standard issue for any circus, this sign was different. In the upper right corner of the sign, in bold black letters was this message: "Featuring Lash LaRue." By nightfall, every youngster in town had been alerted to this upcoming historic event, and children were checking the calendar to be sure that they would be in town. There was no need for me to do that since my availability was never in question. We never went on a vacation, and that was also true of some other families at that time. Nonetheless, I still wrote the great man's name on the appropriate date.

Lash LaRue may not have been as big a star as Roy Rogers or Gene Autry, but unlike them, he never had to resort to a gun to capture the bad guys or to restore peace in the valley. He did not even carry a gun. Lash's weapon of choice was a bullwhip. It was fifteen feet long, and when he cracked it, desperados would cower. Dressed completely in black, he was the original "Man in Black," long before Johnny Cash adopted that image. His horse, Rush, was coal black, and together they enthralled hordes of young moviegoers on Saturday afternoons. Who could forget *Law of the Lash* or *Mark of the Lash*? Had the bad guys been smarter in these movies, they might have figured out that they could have avoided the whip by staying at least sixteen feet away, but fortunately for Lash's fans, bad guys never seemed to think that way.

JAMES LAHIFF

One predictable aftereffect of any Lash LaRue movie would be that many young fans would go home and scrounge up a piece of rope to serve as a whip. It had to be a least four feet long, and clothesline was the popular choice. Most mothers did not respond well upon discovering that their clothesline had been shortened. Kids would play with their "whips" for a few days and forget about them until the next LaRue movie was presented. The cycle would then repeat itself.

Whenever a circus came to town, my friends and I would be at the site by 8:00 a.m. in order to enjoy the activity. The only tent up when we got there would be the kitchen tent for the workers, and the aroma of strong coffee would hang in the air. Before long, however, the real work of assembling the circus would begin, and that is why we got up early. Watching the elephants raise the big top was always memorable, as were the roustabouts who pounded long stakes into the ground to secure the big tent. It was also interesting to see the workers rolling the cages of wild animals into the proper position. It bordered on the miraculous the way a barren field could be transformed into a wonderland in just a few hours.

We had hoped to see Lash or Rush that morning but never got a glimpse of either, and before heading home for lunch we tried to get some inside information from the workers. I asked three roustabouts about Lash and never got a suitable answer. The first man did not seem to understand my question and gave me a blank stare. The second one shrugged his shoulders. Then I changed my approach and asked, "Where can I find Rush?" and the third man, the most loquacious of the trio, said, "Don't know." My friends were equally unsuccessful in trying to resolve the mystery, and we were apprehensive as we rode our bikes home. We were decidedly skeptical as to whether such a great man would actually bother coming to our small town.

We attended the evening performance and were sitting two or three rows above the ground, near the main entrance. There was a big crowd, nearly one thousand people, and since it was a three-ring circus, there was constant activity. After one hour with no sign of the main attraction, we were getting anxious. Monkeys were riding on the backs of ponies in the ring nearest us when the ringmaster blew his whistle. All action stopped and all of the performers, including the pony-riding monkeys, began to exit the big top. The human performers bowed and waved as the crowd applauded in appreciation. The monkeys, however, remained stoic.

The lights then dimmed to near total darkness, and a voice on a loudspeaker said "Ladies and Gentlemen! Cole Brothers Circus is proud to present our featured attraction, Mister Lash LaRue!" A bright spotlight came on and there they were. Rush reared up and Lash cracked his whip twice. The lights returned to normal and Lash rode Rush at a gallop twice around the entire tent, cracking his whip, close enough to the audience that the lower rows got sprayed with sawdust. After that Rush reared up, Lash waved to the crowd, and they departed to great cheering and wild applause. The show continued for another thirty minutes, but we remained awestruck by what we had seen.

Afterward, while my father drove us home, my friends and I evaluated the circus and concurred that it was topnotch. Although none of us had ever seen a circus that we did not like, we felt that this one was truly exceptional, thanks to its main attraction. Somewhat disappointed that Lash's performance had only lasted for about three minutes, we reasoned that it was important for Lash and Rush to avoid any injury that might prevent them from making more movies. For us that was the best three minutes of the night, if not of our lives. There was no doubt that more clotheslines would be cut in the morning.

The Shrine Circus only came to town once while I was young, but it was a memorable experience. It was scheduled to play three afternoon and two evening performances at the high school football field, and the night before the first show, my father got a telephone call from one of the performers, Senor Velasquez, a Spanish horse trainer. Three of his horses were having problems with their shoes and he made an appointment with my father to tend to the horses. It was agreed that he would bring the three horses to the shop on Thursday afternoon after the final performance. I was agog at this brush with greatness.

At noon the next day, my dad gave me a note to deliver to Senor Velasquez, and I raced off to the field. At the front gate I was directed to his trailer and the man who answered my knock read the note, smiled and said, "Yes, I will bring my horses to your shop on Thursday at 5:00," and added, "Why don't you find a seat and stay for the show," and I graciously obliged him. Since the circus was held in the open air, rather than confined by a tent, the aerial acts seemed higher and even more "death defying" than usual. One performer towered over the others as he balanced on a tall, flexible steel pole that swayed in a motion that resembled a windshield wiper at its slowest setting Just when the man appeared likely to plummet to the earth, his muscular tension would force the pole to sway in the opposite direction and back to safety. I could not look away from him, and while I fervently hoped that he would not fall, I was also thinking that if he were destined to fall somewhere, it would be exciting if it were to happen here.

The second day, my father said he had another note for me to take. When Senor Velasquez came to the door, he glanced at the note, laughed and said, "Thursday at 5:00. Right. Find a good seat. Enjoy the show," and, not wishing to offend him, I did. The third day was a repeat of the previous two, but this time Senor shouted, "You again!" and roared with laughter. He did not even glance at the note but said, "Go and find the best seat in the house." When the circus left town, the horses were more comfortable with their shoes and the pole-swaying daredevil, still intact, prepared to thrill another community. It was a long time before it dawned on me what the actual purpose of the notes had been.

It was in late summer that Sis began her campaign to get a dog. At first, I thought that we were about as likely to get a dog as I was to be allowed to attend movies during the season of Lent, but she persisted. The dog she wanted was not just any dog but one that had recently been given to an elderly couple on our street. It was intended to "keep them company," but this couple was spectacularly ill-suited to own a dog. The wife was a nice person who had severe mobility problems and could barely walk. She had not been outdoors in several years. The husband could walk, but only for short distances, and he was further limited by a negative attitude. Simply put, he was grouchy. The prospect of him ever warming up to a dog was unimaginable, and the likelihood of a dog warming up to him even more of a stretch. To top matters off, they were keeping the dog in a garbage can on their back porch.

The picture that Sis presented of the dog's existence was so grim that I had to see it for myself so early the next morning I did. It was every bit as bad as she had described. To the owners' credit, the garbage can was shiny and new, but it was still a corrugated metal can, not designed for canine habitation. The floor of the can was covered by a piece of carpet, and the open top with a framed window screen held in place by a brick. The garbage can was kept on the back porch. Several times each day, the dog was carried into the yard for a few minutes but was immediately placed back into the garbage can. Her living quarters reminded me of solitary confinement as depicted in the prison movies I had seen, and the dog was one pitiful prisoner.

When Sis approached Char about getting a dog, Char did not express an opinion but said, "Talk to your father." He might not have favored the idea, but he recognized the many things that Sis had done for the family since our mother's death, how she had held the family together, and he could not turn her down. Also, he had always liked dogs. As soon as Dad said "Yes" Sis went to the neighbor, and they were so glad to get rid of the unwanted burden that they gave her the dog's leash. She was pleased to have rescued it and delighted to now be a dog owner. No one, however, was more delighted than the dog, free after a month of confinement in a garbage can. She would be restricted to the kitchen and would sleep alongside a radiator on an old folded blanket. Her surroundings were spartan, but compared to her previous residence, of five-star quality.

A golden-colored cocker spaniel, she had not been given a name until Sis announced that its name would be Taffy. Taffy quickly befriended four of our five family members, everyone except my father, whom she stayed as far away from as possible. The more he coaxed her to come to him, the more suspicious and resistant she became. The hard time she had served at her previous residence seemed to have soured her on adult males. When neither cajoling nor pleading swayed her in the least, my father resorted to the ultimate ploy: temptation. He would hold a treat in his hand and extend it toward her, and she would approach, interested but still out of reach. It was almost six weeks before Taffy warmed up to him, and he soon became her favorite person. Several years later when he had a carpenter build a rowboat for the family, the boat was christened Taffy L.

Sister Germaine (born Maria Gerlinski) was my sixth-grade teacher, and she was my favorite. She was young, probably in her twenties, and she was serious about her teaching, but she had a light touch in the way she conveyed information. She made us work hard, but we enjoyed it, and she was interested in our activities away from school.

JAMES LAHIFF

Three neighborhood friends and I would sometimes play football against my classmate Bill and his friends from his neighborhood on Riverside Avenue, the most prestigious street in town. Riverside Avenue was lined with large stately homes, and spacious wooded yards. The current owners were doctors, lawyers, and other professionals, and they enjoyed the same unobstructed view of the river as the lumber barons, who had been the original occupants more than a century earlier. Although it was a short walk from Ludington Street to Riverside Avenue, the status and economic differences between the two neighborhoods were pronounced. Our football games were not exactly the haves versus the have nots, but more like the have-a-lots versus the have-a-littles, and Sister Germaine would seem genuinely interested in the outcome and all the details. She made us think that our games and we, by extension, were quite important. In the early evening, when the weather was mild, she would sometimes roller-skate around the large block that contained the school, church, rectory, and convent. She was not a leisurely skater. She was fast, and when she got up to full speed, her black veil would be streaming behind her, and it made for a memorable sight. Everyone seemed to enjoy the idea of a nun on wheels. She was a genuine memory-maker, and every memory was a positive one.

There was an alley alongside the shop and across the alley, the closest neighbor to the shop, was a wholesale food warehouse. The manager would occasionally offer bargains to my father on food that was not selling well at the stores in the community. One night my dad came home with a case, twenty-four jars, of boysenberry jam, which he had gotten from the warehouse for "practically nothing." Recalling some of the other bargains he had brought home, our expectations were low, but we were pleasantly surprised. The jam had a nice crisp flavor that added zest to our toast at breakfast, and it was tasty in sandwiches after school. We did not realize that boysenberries were a rarity in the Midwest at that time, and that they were grown mainly on the west coast and in New Zealand. The jam may have been delivered to the town by mistake. Nonetheless, we were enjoying the boysenberry jam.

Each jar held twelve ounces of jam, and after two weeks we had already emptied three of the jars. Taffy was told not to beg at the table and she didn't, but she was always available when a morsel fell onto the floor, and it was apparent that she also approved of the boysenberry jam. By the end of the third week, we were no longer slathering the jam onto the toast. We had found that the lightest spread of the jam was sufficient to satisfy our taste buds. It was at about this time that we seemed to begin dropping more scraps of toast, and Taffy continued to excel in her cleanup role. Two weeks later our collective appetite for boysenberry jam had been sated, and Taffy was no longer accepting anything that contained it. A month later, we discovered that the four remaining jars had mysteriously disappeared overnight, and not a complaint was heard nor investigation launched.

Like most boys, I did not pay any attention to my hair until I was nearing high school. There were probably ten barbershops in town, but I continued to go to the one where I had gotten my first haircut. Each time I went there the barber would ask what I wanted, and I would reply, "the usual," and five minutes later I would step down from the chair, hand him a quarter and be on my way. At about this same time there was an up-and-coming singing group, the Crew Cuts (who could forget "Sh-Boom" or "Ko Ko Mo"?), and my age group was becoming more conscious of personal appearance. One day I surprised the barber by asking for a crew cut, and left feeling pleased with myself for my bold move. When I got home, however, I looked in the mirror and was startled by what I saw. My head had the shape of a bowling ball with all the hair the same length. Three weeks later, I went for a haircut and, thinking that the barber had made a mistake last time, I said, "I'll have a crew cut this time," but the result was the same. After three more weeks of living with the bowling ball look, my patience exhausted, I realized that the situation called for immediate action.

Larry's Barber Shop was a few blocks further away, but desperate times do call for desperate measures, even if the price of a haircut there was fifty cents. The shop was most impressive, with bright lights, shiny equipment, and a feel and a smell of newness. Some might call it vanity, but I had resigned myself to the fact that if I wanted to look good it would cost more. As Larry snipped away at my hair, I was confident that I had chosen wisely and that this was the place to get a good crew cut. After he finished, I stepped down from the chair, handed Larry my fifty cents, but my spirits sank when a quick glance in the mirror showed that my head once again had that familiar bowling ball look, identical to the twenty-five cent version. As I was leaving, I noticed a picture on the wall of a man with the type of haircut I had envisioned for myself, and I asked Larry what I would have to do to get a haircut like that. "All you have to do," he said, "is ask for a flattop." A few more questions could have prevented several months of coiffure agony.

Every summer Mister Majors, who owned the print shop next to our house, would plant a vegetable garden behind his shop. The garden was separated from our yard by a wooden fence that was three feet high. One summer there was a bumper crop of tomatoes that Pat, who was as clever as he was bold, could not resist. He found a quart-size tin can, sharpened the edge with a file down at the shop where he then drilled a small hole in the side of the can. Next, he found a stick to fit into the hole to serve as a handle, and he would lean over the fence and gently cut the tomato from the vine, and it would drop into the can. He would wait until Mister Majors had gone home. Once he confronted Pat and said that he knew what was "going on" and told him to "cut it out" or he would be in big trouble. Pat professed his innocence, saying that it must be rabbits, and that was the end of that except for the occasional pilfering which continued until the end of the tomato season. My "clash" with him was much less dramatic, but it occurred more than once. I would sometimes play catch with myself by throwing a tennis ball against the wall of his shop. After a few minutes, he would tap on his window with a broom handle until I stopped. A few days later, the same scene would be repeated. I kept waiting for the day when he would grow immune to the sound of the ball, but that day never came.

Mary Lou, on the other hand, had nothing but positive experiences with him. Whenever our school would conduct a fundraising drive, and such drives were frequent, students were expected to sell some product to their neighbors. Mary Lou's first stop would always be the print shop, and she would always make a sale. She could be selling some unrecognized brand of candy, unappealing peanut brittle, wrapping paper, or holiday cards, perhaps of questionable quality, but he always bought. Pat and I saw him as a crabby guy who did not like children. To Sis he was a nice man and a loyal customer.

When Sis asked me if I would like to learn to play a musical instrument, the thought of it immediately struck a positive chord. Since I had always enjoyed listening to music, there was no reason that making music would not be even more enjoyable. After I assured her that I would practice faithfully, a deal was struck. She purchased a used Selmer alto saxophone for seventy-five dollars from a man who had played it for many years in local dance bands.

Thus began my odyssey into the world of music. Over the next twelve months, I had two different instructors. The first was Bud, a "cool cat" by local standards. In his midthirties, he sold men's clothing in an upscale store, and he was a wizard on the sax. He apparently failed to recognize my potential, however, and after three months he gave me the name of a person who would be "better suited" to work with me. Elmer was older and quieter, a factory worker by day and active on the local music scene. He emphasized the importance of the correct embouchure, the relationship between mouth and mouthpiece, that was essential to develop a good tone. He played a record of Freddy Gardner, a British musician, and his rendition of "Roses of Picardy" to illustrate the vibrato that I should try to develop in my tone. He also identified Johnny Hodges, an American jazz musician, as a model for me to emulate. As soon I began saxophone lessons, I bought a one-year subscription to *Billboard* magazine, a bible of the music business, to help me prepare for the exalted life of a professional musician.

A year earlier, a middle-aged couple had bought the house next door and converted it into a music store with living quarters in the rear. The store emphasized the sale and service of accordions, and the husband gave accordion lessons. With the windows open, we heard the efforts of students at all levels of accomplishment. "Lady of Spain" seemed to be the national anthem of accordionists. My friend Jerry was one of the first students at the new store. He had already been studying the accordion for years, and before long, he was being hired to perform at local bars for eight dollars per night. I envied him for getting paid for doing something that he enjoyed, conveniently overlooking the years of lessons and practice required for him to reach that level. The store also sold sheet music and a variety of accessories, including reeds for saxophones. A reed sold for twenty-five cents, but I was given a special "next-door neighbor discount" and was charged only twenty cents. No matter what type of reed I used, however, the sound I produced resembled the bleating of a constipated sheep. My enthusiasm for having to practice and my one-year subscription to Billboard magazine expired at about the same time.

Though my musical skills were minimal, I was recruited for my high school band. It was a small school, and it had a band to match, eight or nine "musicians." The bar for membership in the band was low since the main requirement was that a person own an instrument, and our signature song was "Pop Goes the Weasel." When played by us, the song was completely devoid of any "pop," and most resembled a poorly played funeral dirge. I enjoyed being a part of the band even though we were rarely invited to perform in public, and when we were there was never a second invitation. Sis was more disappointed than surprised when I quit my music lessons, but she continued to be my biggest supporter.

We never tried to "keep up with the Joneses" but when we got a new Majestic floor model radio-phonograph that was a giant step forward for us in home entertainment. Until then we had a floor model Victrola that played 78-rpm vinyl records. The average 78-rpm record played for less than three minutes so a person would be kept quite busy operating the device. After selecting a record and removing it from its paper envelope, one would place the record on the turntable. Next, use the hand crank that extended out the side of the device to tighten the spring that drives the turntable. Then align the arm holding the needle with the outermost groove on the record, flip the on/off switch, and enjoy the song. None of this constitutes arduous labor, but almost as much time was spent in the preparation as in the enjoyment. Another reason why we did not use it much was that most of the records were from the 1930s. One need not listen to songs like "Beyond the Blue Horizon" and "Happy Days Are Here Again" many times before the songs begin to lose their appeal. Another "favorite" had been Coach Knute Rockne's pep talk to the Notre Dame football team. That was from the 1920s.

The new Majestic phonograph was everything that the Victrola had not been, much more automated, better sound, and much less labor intensive. Not only did it play 33.3 rpm records, one of which would last nearly an hour, it could hold a stack of ten records and changed them automatically. We went from hearing music in three-minute snippets to enjoying hours of it with absolutely no exertion required. Sis was a freshman, in demand as a babysitter, and she enjoyed songs from Broadway musicals. Some of her earnings were spent on original cast recordings of shows such as *Oklahoma* and *South Pacific*. Some nights I would fall asleep with the lyrics of "Surrey with the Fringe on Top" going through my mind, other nights "Some Enchanted Evening." Showtunes made a lasting impression on me.

For one semester during eighth grade, twice each week the class would walk a few blocks for an hour of instruction at the county vocational school. While the girls studied home economics, the boys learned basic woodworking. Mr. Garland, the woodshop instructor, was a patient man whose patience was tested in every class. Following an introduction to the fundamentals of carpentry, we were each assigned a band saw and began working on our projects. Mr. Garland was focused and businesslike, effusive with neither praise nor criticism. He emphasized safety and seemed most intent on insuring that all the students completed the course with the same number of fingers as when they enrolled. When he inspected my first project, a wall shelf, I interpreted his nod to mean "Great job." Several weeks later, after evaluating my second project, a pair of bookends, he said that he had never seen anything quite like them. Rather than ask what he meant by his remark, I felt certain that he thought they were one of a kind, in a class by themselves, in other words terrific. When my final grade for the course did not meet my expectations, I charitably attributed it to human error on Mr. Garland's part. Unfortunately, the ability to accurately evaluate is sometimes lacking in teachers who may be superior in other aspects.

Sports were an important part of high school life, although we were often reminded that academics always came first. Unlike public high school where coaches also taught classes, our coaches had full-time jobs elsewhere, and their backgrounds were varied. Insurance agents, lawyers, and factory workers were among the occupations of individuals who coached our teams. The two major requirements most likely were some experience in having played the sport and a willingness to work for a small amount of money. The coaches seemed motivated by their love for the game; however, after a few seasons they were usually gone.

Pat was muscular and well-coordinated, an excellent football player. He played for all four years of high school. He enjoyed football more than basketball, but he did play basketball in the recreational league at the armory. The name of his team was the BTOs, which meant "big time operators." After he graduated from high school we would sometimes play catch in the gravel road behind our house in his quest to turn me into a football player, and that was fun. Every quest, however well-intended, does not necessarily succeed.

My athletic career was both undistinguished and short-lived. Unlike Pat, I was not a natural athlete. I was scrawny and uncoordinated, but still enjoyed sports. As a freshman, I had no intention of joining the football team until the coach met with me and two other nonparticipants. He talked about the importance of a good football team to represent our school, and he told us that he was "desperate" for more players. I succumbed to his plea and joined the freshman team. It was comprised of approximately fifteen players, and we had a two game schedule. I played quite a bit but did not contribute much, and after the final game the coach thanked me for having joined the team. Although he did not explicitly say it, I got the message that he did not expect to be as desperate next season, and that I should probably look for another sport.

Since only two sports were offered at Lourdes School, my next venture was to try out for the basketball team. I played on the junior varsity, but I spent more time on the bench than on the court. I enjoyed the sport, but there is a big difference between enjoying something and being good at it. It was at about this time that our eye doctor informed me that I had amblyopia (lazy eye), a condition that, unless it was corrected before age seven or eight, would leave a person with only one good eye. Common side effects were faulty depth perception and possible clumsiness. At last, I knew why I was such a mediocre athlete, or so I thought. Since then I have read several articles in newspapers and magazines about people in a wide variety of occupations, including athletics, who experienced much success even though they had amblyopia. Sometimes it is wise to know when to quit reading.

As a freshman, I joined the staff of *The Lourdes*, the monthly school newspaper, and as my future in sports turned bleaker my prospects in journalism grew brighter. For three years I wrote a column, "Out on a Limb with Jim," in which I discussed the weighty issues of school and country, but especially of school. Also, singing in the glee club and participating in regional competitions was fun even if we were often reminded how average we were. Our rendition of "The Donkey Serenade," however, was a surefire crowd-pleaser, no matter what the judges thought. The pleasure of overacting in plays was heightened by the absence of judges. These activities created a comfortable and enjoyable niche during four years of high school.

At the (S)hop

My father, Alvin Joseph Lahiff, usually called Al or A.J., was a blacksmith in a business that his father had started in 1881. Immediately after high school he began working in the shop and in 1924, when his father died, he took over the business. A blacksmith was an important part of society in early America and for centuries before that. Until the Industrial Revolution in the late 1800s, anything made of iron would have to be made by a blacksmith, and for that reason, there were many of them. Marinette and Menominee, two small towns, had ten of them at the turn of the nineteenth century. When my father died in 1969, he was the last blacksmith in either town. In early England, the name Smith meant a person who worked with metal, and the prevalence of that name today suggests how many blacksmiths there once were.

The original blacksmith shop was built by my grandfather, and my father did business there for approximately twenty-five years. The building was beyond dilapidated. Made of wood with a faded blue exterior, badly in need of repainting, the building was rectangular in shape. The roof sagged and the building leaned slightly toward the south. The north winds coming off the river, one block away, probably contributed greatly to the southerly lean. Several decades earlier, the building might have been considered a fixer-upper, but it was far beyond that; it was now a tearer-downer. In addition to its cosmetic defects, the only attempt to insulate was a partition made of cardboard that divided the shop into two equal sections. The flimsy partition was there to keep the heat from escaping into the rear of the shop, but there was never much heat to escape. A potbellied stove was the main source of heat, but it was not up to the challenge presented by the typical five months of Wisconsin cold weather. The frigidity of the concrete floor contributed an additional layer of discomfort. A sign on the wall said, "Need Credit? Visit Our Credit Department. Please Take Elevator." It was a one-story building.

One reason that my father decided to build a new shop was because the old one had become a real fire hazard. Considering the age of the wooden structure, and the prevalence of flames, sparks, and hot embers in any blacksmith shop, it was surprising that the building had not burned down long ago. The new shop, slightly smaller than the original, had walls made of cinder blocks, a concrete floor, and a flat wooden roof covered with tar. On the front, there was an oversize garage door that was large enough to accommodate trucks. The new shop was located directly across the street from its predecessor on property already owned by my father.

He had been urged to have a modern heating system installed, but he would have none of that. He moved the potbellied stove over from the original shop, content with the same meager heat he had gotten used to. On cold mornings, he would start a fire with two large chunks of soft coal, and the stove would provide some warmth to anyone no further than three feet away. When he worked on the forge, there would be some warmth, but many days he did not spend much time at the forge or close to the stove. It was a bone-chilling cold place and he dressed appropriately. He would usually wear a wool shirt with a denim jacket over that and a mackinaw over that. His work shoes came from the Knapp Company and had double soles and steel toes. Despite the steel toes, however, he suffered a broken toe, two successive years on Friday the thirteenth, when a piece of steel fell on his foot. When the weather was mild, there would be a steady stream of customers with work and visitors coming in to socialize. During the months of January and February, there would only be customers with urgent projects, and they would not linger.

The basics of any blacksmith shop would include a forge, an anvil, and a slack tub, and this shop had that and much more. There was a drill press mounted on the wall, a large shear cutter stood on the floor, worktables with vises, a gas welder, an electric welder, and hand tools of every size and shape. To an outsider the shop appeared completely disorganized, but my father knew where everything was. It was a fascinating place and a person could rummage around in it for hours, but that person would probably be very dirty upon emerging. Coal ash from the forge would settle on any stationary object, like a coat of dust.

Throughout history, blacksmiths were known for their broad set of skills that allowed them to perform a wide variety of tasks. That is why their shops were usually located near the center of a town, so they would be equally accessible to everyone. My father was well known for the ornamental wrought iron railings that he made. He usually installed them on front porches and occasionally in places of business, and they could be seen throughout the community. In the summer, from our house, I could often hear the clang of his hammer while he reshaped red-hot iron on his anvil.

The length of a railing usually depended on the size of the front porch, and that was based on the size of the house to which it was attached. His longest railing was the one he made for the Moses Montefiore Synagogue in downtown Marinette. Approximately thirty feet long, it was in the shape of a trapezoid, designed to accommodate nine steps on each side of the concrete porch, as well as the large flat surface outside the entry. In the middle of the railing was a Star of David. For most railings, he measured once and did the job. In this instance, he went back a second time and remeasured to be sure. Every railing he ever made fit perfectly into the predrilled holes in concrete surfaces.

It would be impossible to list all the different objects he produced in his shop, but there were several that he made frequently enough to merit mention. Since Marinette is situated both on a major river (Menominee) and on Lake Michigan, boating, recreational and commercial, is a major activity. My father made many iron cleats, devices which were bolted onto docks for boats to tie up to. He made them in different sizes, appropriate for residential docks and smaller boats, municipal marinas for yachts and sailboats, or commercial docks where large ships such as iron ore carriers would dock.

Another product he developed was a ceiling-mounted pots and pans rack for the local F W Woolworth store. A Woolworth store, often called a "Five and Dime" was a prominent retailer in most cities and towns. There were thousands of them in the US, and most had a lunch counter and a small kitchen. My father designed and created an iron rack three feet long and ten inches wide, shaped like a rectangle with rounded ends and ten hooks on it to hang cooking utensils. The rack would hang from the ceiling and the pots and pans would be within reach of the cooks, but out of the way until needed. Word of the device spread among the Woolworth managers, and he produced approximately twenty of them.

The trailer hitches that he made were stronger and safer than those available in stores at that time. While most trailer hitches were simply clamped to the rear bumper of a car, his were made of heavier steel and welded to the underbody of the vehicle. Today one can order such devices as a kitchen rack, a dock cleat, or a trailer hitch from a catalogue, but it was not always that way. Much of his work required a high degree of precision, and he was very good with numbers.

In later years, as more products were being mass-produced, he devoted less time to making things and more time to repairing them. One day it would be a farmer with a broken farm implement, and the next day a housewife bringing in her child's tricycle, badly twisted and flattened after she drove over it in her driveway.

As was true of many blacksmiths, he also made horseshoes and shoed horses. Oftentimes, he would go out to farms to do that, but when the horse was brought to the shop, interested onlookers were guaranteed. Dr. Koepp, a local MD, would often walk past the shop on his way back to his clinic after lunch. As he expressed it, "Whenever Al Lahiff had a horse in his shop, I knew I'd be late for my 1:30 appointment."

It takes approximately one hour to shoe a horse, and during that time, the farrier follows the same steps with each hoof. The old shoe is removed, and a short-handled curved knife is used to remove extraneous matter from the bottom of the hoof. The new shoe is attached to the hoof by seven or eight horseshoe nails that are driven through the outer edge of the bottom of the hoof. The farrier then lifts the hoof onto a low stool and uses a pliers-like clipper to cut off most, but not all, of each nail protruding through the top of the hoof. The nail stubs are then bent over with a hammer, and those bent stubs help hold the shoe in place. Lastly, with the hoof still on the stool, a heavy iron rasp would be used to file any rough edges from the nails and to trim the edges of the hoof. Then it is on to the next hoof.

Shoeing horses requires skill and strength, and no two horses are alike. Some horses, while being shod, are comfortable standing on three legs and will apply little weight to the back of the farrier. Others treat the farrier as a fourth leg and put their full weight on his back. Many of the horses that my father shod were draft horses, used for pulling heavy loads and plowing fields. Draft horses are big, muscular, and often weigh a ton or more. Having to remain in an uncomfortable position, bent over with a heavy weight on his back while working on a hoof was hard work. My father charged seventy-five cents per hoof.

Whenever he drove to a farm to shoe horses, it would be at the end of his normal workday, usually after supper, and sometimes I would accompany him. It was always interesting to get a glimpse of what life on a farm was like and to see all the hard work that was required to run a farm. On one visit, the horse being shod was tied to a wooden fence, twenty feet long and supported by three posts that were driven into the ground. The horse was suddenly spooked by a cat running beneath it and reared up, pulling the entire fence out of the ground. Moments like that were a reminder of how unpredictable horses could be.

Once he was hired to shoe more than a dozen riding horses at a ranch owned by a wealthy family from Chicago, a family made wealthy by their chewing gum business. Since the ranch was located approximately fifty miles away, he planned to divide the job over two days, and I accompanied him. We slept in the bunkhouse, and ate with the farmhands. The property was sprawling, and I had never seen anything like it. There was a landing strip for small planes, a lake, riding trails, and large fields of crops. I spent much of the time riding a pony around a big field, never far out of my father's sight. Being ten years old, I found it fun on the first day and somewhat boring as the second day dragged on. I think that the pony felt the same way. Having already visited a fair number of farms, I learned that day that not all farms are created equal.

The variety of jobs my father did was exceeded only by the variety of people who stopped at the shop and the subjects that were discussed. When the weather was mild the shop's front door, an oversize garage door, would be open and there would be a steady stream of visitors, a few of whom would be actual customers. Some people would come to watch what Dad was doing and others to find out what was going on downtown, and the shop was the place to find that out.

Children, especially boys, would be attracted to the shop by the noise, sparks, and level of activity, but my father would urge them to go home.

Sometimes it took a tall tale to get them moving. He once asked a small group of boys if they had heard about the Russian submarine that had been captured in the bay. Their eyes widened as he described it as half the length of a football field and shaped like a rocket. He told them that it was tied up at the coal dock, and he suggested that they ask their father to take them to see it. The fathers would visit the shop soon thereafter with variations of, "Damn it, Al, my kid nagged me until I drove him down to the coal dock," or "I missed my nap yesterday because of you." He was serious about his work, but he also had a sense of humor.

Local politics was a popular topic of conversation at the shop. For example, when the city council announced that the city needed a new fire engine the news was met with howls of protest. Many called it "another waste of money." Almost everyone who came into the shop felt that there was no need for a new fire truck but after two weeks recognized that the purchase was inevitable. Next, the city council, with urging from the city manager, selected one of the more expensive models, and the outcry from the crowd at the blacksmith shop reached even higher decibels. Two weeks after the delivery of the new fire truck, the city manager bought a new Buick, and that "coincidence" remained the hot topic for the next several months.

People especially liked to complain about taxes, as well as the suspected malfeasance of public officials. Potholes were another popular topic of conversation. Ice, snow, and extremely low temperatures damaged roads and made road maintenance challenging. The glories of springtime would always be accompanied by a prevalence of holes in the surface of the roads. Comments at the shop suggested that there were two types of potholes: Those that jarred the skeletal system of both driver and vehicle with each encounter and should have been repaired weeks ago, and those whose repair was so shoddy that future problems were guaranteed. Sometimes the Green Bay Packers would be the topic, but at that time the Packers were a source of ridicule rather than pride. A discussion might morph into an argument, and voices would rise, but people were always civil to one another, and swearing was virtually nonexistent. Persons who had been involved in a vehement argument one day would return a few days later with no apparent recollection of their recent difference of opinion. There was, however, an occasional exception.

Until his retirement from his railroad job, Ed would stop in the shop every few months. After he retired, he visited more frequently, at least once a week. Ed was a lifelong Democrat, a strong union supporter, and a Protestant. My father was a conservative Republican, suspicious of unions, and a Catholic. Their relationship was more prickly than amiable but they had always managed to get along, at least until early November of 1959 when Ed said that he intended to vote for Richard Nixon, a Republican. My dad asked him, "How can you vote for Nixon? You're a Democrat." Ed then asked my father who he was voting for, and my father told him that he planned to vote for John Kennedy, who was a Democrat and a Catholic. Ed asked him, "How can you vote for Kennedy? You're a Republican." The conversation went downhill from that point. Ed stomped out, and they did not speak to each other for a long time. One day, approximately a year later, Ed returned to the shop. No mention was ever made of their kerfuffle. It was as though it had never happened, and Ed once again became a regular visitor.

My father always tried to accommodate his customers, and he often had to go out of his way to do so. One man, however, made a request that my dad immediately rejected, but eventually the man made an offer that was too good to refuse. Mr. Elrod owned a granite quarry that was approximately sixty miles away, and a piece of heavy equipment was broken and needed to be welded. The cost of bringing it to the shop would be prohibitive, and his prosperous business would remain shut down until the equipment was repaired. My father felt that positioning his gas welder close enough to do the job would be difficult, and he also had safety concerns. Mr. Elrod was desperate after my dad had turned down two generous offers, and then he made a third offer.

Mr. Elrod owned ten lots of waterfront property, each with one hundred feet of shoreline on the bay. The price he was asking for each lot was much higher than my father could have ever afforded, but Mr. Elrod offered him a deal. If he would agree to do the job, he could select a waterfront lot and set the price he would pay for it. My father agreed and paid a small fraction of the asking price. The granite quarry was soon back in operation, and we owned a wooded lot with one hundred feet of shoreline. That is how my father was able to buy the lot on which our cottage would eventually be built.

As soon as he received the deed for the property, he had several trees removed, trees that would have blocked the driveway that he envisioned. For the next two years, on one or two nights each week, except when the snow was too deep, he and I would drive out to the lot with a load of cinders in his two-wheeled wooden trailer. We used the cinders to build a driveway from the main road to the spot where the cottage would eventually be constructed. The cinders came from a small coal-fired furnace at the Valeteria Dry Cleaners, which was immediately adjacent to the Knight Kap, another neighbor of the shop. The man who owned the cleaners was happy to have us take the cinders rather than have to dispose of them himself.

The driveway was to be approximately twenty yards long, and building it turned out to be a slow process since each trailer-load of cinders was the equivalent of only seven- or eight-bushel baskets. In my mind, the driveway would consist of a light sprinkling of cinders. In my father's mind, it would be four or five inches deep, built to last. We went with my father's version. I was skeptical, a real naysayer, like the experts who said that the Panama Canal could never be built. I doubted that we could ever complete what I regarded as an insurmountable task. Unlike the Canal naysayers, however, I kept my opinion to myself. I was more of a naythinker. Too young to be of much help, my main function was to provide company, and to help tamp the cinders into the ground. There would usually be news on the car radio for the five-mile trip out, and we would not talk much. On the return trip, there would be a disc jockey playing records, and my father might comment on the music. He liked Frankie Laine, Tennessee Ernie Ford, and Johnny Cash, but he did not care for Frank Sinatra.

Soon after the driveway was completed, Pat and his future wife, Joanne Weber, built a tool shed out of used lumber. The unpainted shed had a sloping roof, a door that locked, and it rested on cinder blocks. A thing of beauty it was not, but it served its purpose for more than twenty years, as did the cinder driveway. Two years after the driveway was completed the cottage was built.

Biding My Time

Monday was washday for most families, and it was a labor-intensive process that would take at least a half day. Our Maytag washing machine, located toward the front of the basement, was a close second in importance to the furnace. The washing machine stood alongside a large sink, and a hose connected to a faucet on the sink provided the water. The machine was drained through a spigot at the bottom of the washer into a bucket, which you then emptied into the sink. The washday ordeal would begin with separating items on the basis of color and dirtiness. There were usually multiple loads of laundry to be washed, and several changes of water were often necessary to get the job done. The washing machine had a wringer attached, which would squeeze water out of the washed clothes, but each item had to be fed individually into the wringer. The wringer could be hazardous to one's digital health, and there were many stories about careless individuals whose fingers got caught in a wringer. It would be some time before they would do much finger pointing. Next, the clean clothes would be hung on the clothesline to dry, either in the backyard or in the basement, depending on the weather. The weather forecaster on the radio would often mention whether it was a good day for drying laundry outdoors.

Doing the wash was hard work, both in time spent and effort expended, and it was often a day of frayed nerves and short tempers for those involved. It was also the worst day of the week for a child to seek a favor or to whine about some grievance. Children would learn early in life that it was wise to maintain a low profile on washday.

A YOUNG LIFE IN YOUR HANDS

It was widely known that most kids who lived on farms had a heavy workload at home, and it was widely believed by those same kids that anyone who lived in town had it much easier. While it is true that we never had to milk cows at 5:00 in the morning or shovel manure out of the barn after school or slop the hogs, most of my friends had certain chores to perform, just as we did.

At age seven or eight, I became the go-to person when it came to running to the store for an item or two. There was no public proclamation issued. nor did I need to pass an exam. One day Char said, "Oh, Jimmy, run and get a can of green beans," and she handed me a few coins and a slip of paper with "one can of green beans" written on it in case I forgot, or perhaps returned with a bag of candy by mistake. I was thunderstruck with the awesome responsibility but quickly recovered, and I was out the door in an instant. At last, I had a mission in life. I did not have to ask which store since the A&P was only two doors away, and I knew that we gave them all our business. That was probably my first chore, and I would repeat it numerous times. During the next five years, I went to the A&P more days than I did not, and I became somewhat of a fixture, known to all the employees. When a young man in the produce department was drafted into the army and sent to Europe to fight in the war, I worried along with the employees and, like them, was relieved when he returned home safely.

At or about age fifteen, Pat got a part-time job with the Allard News Agency, a magazine distributor, after being recommended for it by the principal of our school. Pat never understood why she recommended him since he was no more than an average student, and that was on his better days. At that time, magazines were widely read and available at many stores. His job required him to ride along with a driver, deliver that week's new magazines, and retrieve those that had not been sold. Then he would remove the title from the cover of every unsold magazine, and the titles would be sent to the publisher as evidence that they were not sold. Before Pat got his job the current reading materials in our house consisted of the *Marinette Eagle-Star*, *Reader's Digest*, *Women's Day*, and at times, the *Chicago Tribune*. After Pat got the job, we were reading *Saturday Evening Post*, *Life*, *Look*, *Colliers*, and other magazines. Every cover may have lacked its title and the contents may have been a week old, but we all enjoyed them, and they helped me hone my reading skills.

JAMES LAHIFF

In 1830, Edwin Budding, an Englishman, invented the lawnmower. Until then the few people who cared about the length of their grass had relied upon sheep, goats, or other livestock to do the job, and a fine job they reportedly did. Not only that, the animals reportedly enjoyed doing that job, but Mr. Budding, for whatever reason, felt compelled to replace a perfect system with one that displeased both the out-of-work animals and the boys who would be stuck with the job for evermore. While our lawnmower was probably not a Budding original, it was most likely a close relative. It was a push mower with a wooden T-shaped handle, and it was so old that the brand name was no longer visible, worn away either by the ravages of time or by the embarrassment of its own woeful condition. The wheels revolved grudgingly whether the grass was long or short, and the mower blades would miss as much grass as they would cut. It was often necessary to give the grass a second cutting before it looked reasonable.

When Pat entered the magazine business, I became the family grasscutter. Our house was centered on the property, so the patches of grass (I hesitate to call it a lawn) were identical on both sides of the house, approximately forty feet long and twelve feet wide. The west side of the house bordered Majors' Print Shop. The building was two stories tall, covered with brown tin siding, and its two windows were too high to look into. Our two-story house was built on a high foundation, and cutting grass between the two tall structures was not only boring, but it always felt confining. All there was to look at were the backs of several small stores and Smitty's Ambassador tavern. Since I usually cut the grass around 8:00 in the morning, there was little activity, not even at Smitty's, which did not open until 10:00 a.m.

When I pushed the mower over to the other side of our house, it was like entering a different country, a country devoid of the serenity experienced moments earlier. Our neighbor's house was old, small, and weathered. The wooden siding had not been painted in decades. A father lived there with his daughter, and there was a small garden behind the house. In my eyes, the occupants were both ancient, but George was probably seventy-five, and Gladys in her midfifties. What made the east side so lively was the fact that George and Gladys seemed not to agree on anything, and they argued loudly all day long. Sometimes it was about who would go to the store. Other times what should be bought at the store. Whose turn it was to tend to the garden was another popular topic.

No matter what the topic was, however, Gladys would manage to link it to the amount of liquor that George drank, which to her way of thinking was too much. George would shout back his disagreement and claim that he drank an appropriate amount considering his age and his health. Some might consider their behavior to be bickering or squabbling, but regardless of what it was called, it went on all day. The antics of George and Gladys provided an entertaining soundtrack for me as I cut the grass. Since the mower was powered by hand, rather than by a motor, it made little noise, and I did not miss many words. The more interesting the "discussion," the more slowly I would push the mower.

The corner house was situated on a larger lot than was our family house, and there was more grass to cut. The cutting experience there lacked the drama provided by George and Gladys; however, a higher level of activity compensated for that. The house was located at a busy intersection, with my grandmother's house, a lumber yard, and a Scott Paper converting plant occupying the other corners. While the designation "converting plant" might have religious overtones, there were no souls being saved there. Huge rolls of paper, produced at a mill one mile away, were being converted into family-size packages of toilet paper, tissue, and paper towels. Until 1930, the building had housed the Victory Bag Company, and many older people still called it the Victory Bag.

The converting plant occupied a third of our block in a stone building that was three stories tall, and it operated sixteen hours a day, five days a week, except for a few predictable holidays. Although the converting process was not especially noisy, there was a steady hum emitted by the many machines, a hum that neighbors were reminded of only when the plant shut down. While the plant could not be considered a beehive of activity, except for when the work shifts were changing, there were enough persons entering or exiting the building to capture my attention, to the detriment of my grass cutting. Sometimes one of the tenants might stop and say a word of encouragement such as "Good job," but more often it was "It's about time," or "I hope you'll do a better job this time." It was common knowledge that the tenants were complainers. When I inherited this job from Pat, he told me not to take anything they said seriously. I always admired his attitude, but I had a difficult time making it my own. The tenants saved their major complaints, however, for my father since his shop was conveniently close, and he would occasionally actually act on their wishes.

Until I reached the age at which I could be assigned chores, I could not wait until I was able to do the tasks that Pat or Sis routinely did. It was not long after reaching that threshold that I realized how good I had had it, but there was no returning to yesterday. There was one chore that I was able to avoid doing until I was twelve or thirteen years old, when neither of my siblings were as readily available. The process of wallpaper removal sounded like drudgery to me, and that accurately described it. When a tenant moved out of an apartment, the wallpaper would often be changed to "freshen up the place." Dad, Char, and I would typically work for three hours on two consecutive nights to remove the wallpaper of an average-size room. First, the floor had to be covered with enough newspapers to protect it from the wet mess soon to fall on it. We would each have a bucket of warm water mixed with vinegar, a sponge, and a small handheld scraper. When we rubbed the wet sponge across a small area of the wall, the paper and the glue beneath would eventually become pliable enough to be removed from the plaster wall with the scraper. Progress would be incremental, but unless all traces of paper and glue were eliminated, evidence of shoddy workmanship would be apparent in the texture of whatever new wallpaper would soon grace that wall. This chore required patience and neatness, two virtues I was somewhat lacking. That may explain why my help was never sought when the time came to hang the new wallpaper.

The change of seasons meant different things to different people. In the spring, farmers plowed their fields, and major league baseball teams prepared for the season opener. The spring was the season in which we removed the storm windows and put up the window screens. In the fall, while farmers were harvesting their crops and many birds were flying south, that was when we reversed the process, replacing the window screens with storm windows. At that time, the frames for storm windows and screens were made of solid wood, much heavier than modern frames made of aluminum. Dealing with windows on the first floor only required a stepladder and was relatively easy. A longer ladder, leaning against the house, was needed for the windows on the second floor, however, and that was more challenging, especially when putting the storm windows on. The month would be November, and there would be blustery north winds. With one hand grasping a rung, the other hand attempting to push the storm window up the ladder, and the winds trying to stymie my efforts by stealing the storm window from my hand, I found it an exciting experience. In the spring, the process was much less dramatic because the weather would be more cooperative.

As a small child, I was happy to hear the rumble of snowplows in the early morning darkness. That sound told me that there had been a snowfall of at least three or four inches, and my first wish would be that it be "good packing" snow, the kind that was useful for making snowballs, snowmen, or snow forts. Dunlap Square, the center of downtown, was always the first area to be plowed. It was only a half block from our house, and that sound served as my early alert system. By the time I was ten or eleven, older and wiser, that rumble no longer conveyed glad tidings, but just the opposite, and a light and fluffy snowfall would suit me fine.

While Inuit people are reported to use many different words for snow, my classification system was much simpler. Snow was either powdery or it was wet. Powdery snow was easier to shovel, but more likely to blow into drifts. Wet snow was heavier and harder to shovel, and if not removed promptly would leave a cover of ice on the sidewalk. The ice cover would have to be chipped and scraped off with the shovel, and that could be a time-consuming chore.

There were two sidewalks at our house, one in the front and another that ran the length of the house, alongside the print shop. The front walk was more important since it was heavily used by people going to the A&P or downtown. That would be the first sidewalk that we would clear. Either my father, Pat, or I would be the shoveler, depending upon the circumstances.

The sidewalk at the corner house was considerably longer, and there were also two shorter sidewalks extending from the street to the house. An obstacle to rapid shoveling was a concrete retaining wall, fifteen inches high, that bordered the main sidewalk and supported the lawn, which was fifteen inches above the sidewalk. In the early 1900s, the corner house was probably quite elegant, and the raised lawn was a fashionable feature.

Now the once-proud house, like the other houses on the block, was slowly approaching shabbiness on the road to dilapidation, but the retaining wall, still upright and stable, continued to retain the lawn as well as to be an impediment to any shoveler. Since shoveling snow into the street was frowned upon, one had to shovel it onto the raised lawn, and it would take longer than otherwise. Another problem with the retaining wall was that blowing snow would drift against it. More than once, I cleared the sidewalk in the late afternoon after school only to find it covered with snowdrifts the next morning. Adding to the frustration, the snowdrifts would usually be higher than the original snowfall had been.

Every day from October until May, we filled the stokers in the two houses with coal, and the furnaces provided heat and hot water. At the corner house, the end of the heating season marked the end of a regular supply of hot water. During the warmer months, when the furnace did not operate, hot water would be provided only on Saturday afternoons. At age twelve, I became the provider, just as Pat and Sis had been in earlier years. Until then, I had paid little attention to their grumbling about the "little stove," but after a day or two as the hot water provider, I joined the ranks of grumblers.

Hot water was a luxury, and some families' only option was to heat it in pots and pans on the stove. For that reason, many people bathed only once a week, and Saturday was the traditional bath day. It was not unusual for an entire family to use the same bathwater. Having access to hot water for only a few hours each week was not desirable, but it was not uncommon at that time. Trying to keep the eight or nine tenants satisfied with their share of the water was next to impossible.

The tenants at the corner house were people on tight budgets. They lived there because the rent was cheap. If they had had more money, they would have found accommodations elsewhere, probably in a place that included hot water at all times. A week consists of 168 hours, and when hot water is available for only eight of those hours, it rightfully becomes a precious commodity. If it was unavailable or not hot enough during that significant period of time, there would be complaints followed by more complaints.

The source of the problem, the dastardly "little stove," stood three feet high and two feet wide, and it was made of cast iron. It had two doors in the front, the upper one opening into the firebox where paper, wood, and coal, were placed upon a grate. The lower door was used to extract the ashes. Between the two doors was a detachable handle to be used for shaking the grate in order to dislodge cinders and ashes, which would then be placed into a metal container and discarded. The handle was detachable because the stove would get too hot to touch with bare hands. On the stovepipe leading to the chimney was a handle intended to regulate the "draft," the flow of air allowed into the firebox. There was a cylinder-shaped water tank, five feet high, connected to the stove. By rubbing my hand along the outside of the tank, I could estimate how much hot water there was, and thus the likelihood that tenants would be complaining.

If it were possible for an inanimate object to possess an attitude, the word "surly" would best describe the attitude of the stove. If I happened to be in a hurry, that would be when the task would require prolonged attention. Many times after building what I considered a raging inferno, I would return an hour later to find that the fire had died, leaving unburned coal as its surviving relatives. Any attempt to regulate the flow of air by using the draft handle would have little effect on the flames. In addition to being surly, the stove also seemed contemptuous of my efforts. On a good day, I would devote fewer than ten minutes to each of my hourly visits, but good days were in the minority. For one six-month period, during which a young family lived in the house, someone stored a small stack of men's magazines in the basement, and that made the chore more tolerable. When the family moved away, however, the magazines went with them.

The corner house consisted of a two-bedroom apartment and a one-bedroom apartment on the first floor. On the second floor, there were three single rooms that might charitably be called studio apartments except for the fact that none of them had a bathroom. The lone bathroom on the second floor was down the hall. The upstairs tenants were usually elderly women, strangers to each other, and they shared the bathroom. The competition for hot water could get spirited, and on several occasions, harsh words were exchanged.

Rent was due on the first day of the month, and the tenants would come to our house and pay Char, usually in cash, since few people had checking accounts at that time. When the downstairs tenants came, they would have little to say, but the upstairs renters were more talkative, especially when the weather was warm and the main topic would be hot water or the lack thereof. Not only did each person feel that she was not getting her fair share of the hot water, but she also knew who was to blame. Mrs. Adams said that Mrs. Banks filled the bathtub too high, and Mrs. Cook blamed Mrs. Adams for always wasting water. Char would tell them that if they waited a little longer and allowed more water to heat, there would be enough for everyone. Each person claimed to do exactly that, but they maintained that no one else would follow their good example. Sometimes they would speculate on why the other persons behaved as they did. Conspiracy theories existed long before they were identified as such. The accusations might differ slightly from one month to the next, but they were always conveyed in "I really shouldn't say this" tone. More often than not, the first day of the month could be counted on to provide some drama.

With one exception, the upstairs tenants had always been elderly. That exception was Darlene. She was in her early twenties and had been born and raised on a farm out in the county. She decided that she wanted to try "city life" and found a job operating a sewing machine at a glove factory, located two blocks from the corner house. After her first month as a tenant, both of her neighbors complained that she was too noisy, and Char promised to talk to her about it. Following the second month, they complained that she would sometimes allow her boyfriend to spend the night with her, and they registered their strong disapproval. "You should not be renting to people like that" was the general theme of their complaints, although they were much more verbose in expressing themselves, and one of them implied that she was thinking of moving out. Again, Char assured them that she would talk to her and she did. When Darlene came to pay her rent, she and Char had a chat over a cup of coffee, and Darlene said that she would try to change her ways. The complaints, along with threats to move out, continued, as did the monthly visits over coffee. Char found that she liked Darlene and also felt sorry for her. After ten months, Darlene moved out of her own accord, leaving her neighbors with one less thing to complain about.

Heigh-Ho, Heigh-Ho

When I was in seventh grade, I applied for the job of "newsboy" with the *Marinette Eagle-Star*. I could envision myself delivering newspapers to appreciative persons, eager to read the news that was "hot off the press." I considered it an important job, and I was anxious to get started. Unfortunately, there were no routes available, but I was given the phone number of a carrier who was seeking a helper. Randy was a junior at Marinette High School, and he interviewed me over the phone in a crisp, businesslike manner. The interview consisted of two hard-hitting questions: "What is your name?" and "Can you start tomorrow?" I aced the interview and was immediately hired.

For the next two days, in the late afternoon, I accompanied Randy on his route and learned the ins and outs of the newspaper business. He pointed out the houses of subscribers who could be difficult, as well as those who presented collection problems. My plan was to write what seemed most important in a pocket-size notebook as we walked along, but Randy spoke much faster than I could write so I soon resorted to Plan B and tried to listen intently. When that proved unsuccessful, I wound up learning through Plan C, that old standby, trial and error. Some subscribers were very precise in where they expected to find the paper, and if dissatisfied they would complain to the office. Carriers dreaded being reprimanded by someone from the front office. There were stories about carriers who experienced the wrath of the front office for some transgression; however, no one was ever able to attach a name to a story. In fact, it was unclear if any of the carriers had ever been in the front office. Randy delivered the paper six days per week to approximately fifty houses, and his route was near the *Eagle-Star* office, thus, only a few blocks from my house.

One or two nights each week, Randy would phone and tell me that I was to deliver the paper the next day. He would also tell me the addresses at which money was owed and ask me to try to collect from them. A one-year subscription cost fifteen dollars, but most people paid by the week. Those who were paid up would be happy to see me, anxious to get the paper since it was the main source of news. Those who were behind in their payments tended to be elusive. Randy's policy was to stop delivering to anyone who was two weeks in arrears, and after a few days without a paper, it was customary for most derelicts to pay what they owed, but not without grumbling. "I don't know why I subscribe when all you print is bad news" was a common complaint.

The man who distributed the papers to the carriers was the father of one of my classmates. Each time he handed me my allotment, he would say, in a voice too soft to be heard by others, that he had included two extra copies. In an equally soft voice, I would thank him, although I never understood what I was to do with the extras. Randy had been delivering papers for two years, and I had been assisting him for six months, when he decided to bow out of the newspaper business. He sold his route to a cousin who lacked the wisdom to recognize the value of a knowledgeable and experienced assistant. A short time later, while discussing my abbreviated career in journalism with Pat, I told him how I was always given two extra papers. When I told him that I would give the extras to people who didn't subscribe, he scoffed and said that I should have sold them for five cents each. I had never thought of that. An entrepreneur I was not.

When I was fourteen years old, my father came home for dinner one day and announced that he had found me a job. Until then, I hadn't realized that I had been on the job market, but I was flattered that people were already clamoring for my services. The owner of a hardware store had come to the shop and asked if I would like to work at his store, and my father told him that I certainly would. A deal was made. I would work every Saturday from 8:00 a.m. until 5:00 p.m., and I would be paid thirty-five cents per hour. No more Saturday afternoon bouts with the little stove for me since I would have a real job earning real money. My father's plan was to handle the hot water stove himself since the shop was so close to the corner house. After a few months of coping with the stove, he replaced it with an electric water heater.

The hardware store was across the street from our house, its back door approximately one hundred yards from our front door, separated only by a street and a parking lot. I had never paid much attention to Pioneer Hardware, even though I had been inside it many times, but always to use it as a shortcut to Main Street and Lauerman's Department Store, "Largest Small-City Store in America." During the eighteen months that I worked at the Pioneer, I learned that the number of people who used the store as a shortcut far exceeded the number of people who shopped there.

The Pioneer was situated in the middle of a long block of businesses, between a tavern (Ambassador) and Marlane's Beauty Parlor. Although small in size, the store offered many goods, including housewares and appliances of all types. In the rear was a repair shop. Mainly, however, it was a traditional well-stocked hardware store. Due to space limitations, merchandise was stacked along the walls, almost as high as the pressed tin ceiling. To a newcomer, the store might appear disorganized, but the opposite was true. Its haphazard appearance resulted from the extensive variety of products offered. There were not many stores where a person could buy a clothes dryer, a lazy susan, machine bolts, and mousetraps, all under the same roof.

In addition to the owner, there were three other employees. Fred, jovial, talkative, and in his early thirties, was a person who seemed pleased with his sales position and with his life. Dennis, the appliance repairman, was a recent high school graduate and former football star. He was more serious, and he was intently looking for a better job. Betty, a solemn twenty-two-year-old, was the part-time bookkeeper. Her work area was on a raised wooden platform, accessible by six steps, in the rear of the store. The platform was cramped with two desks, a file cabinet, and a typewriter stand. Quiet and conscientious, she would never participate in any occasional joking that might transpire, and she seemed like a person ready to get up and run out the door the moment she received an offer for another job.

When things were quiet at the store, as they often were, Fred would try to liven things up with his stories and jokes, of which he had an endless supply. He also enjoyed playing pranks on people, and I was the victim of one when he announced that he had inventoried the rope supply and discovered that we were completely out of shore line. He asked me to go to the hardware department at Lauerman's and buy one hundred feet of it. When I attempted to make the purchase, the clerk smiled and said that they also were out of it and suggested that I try Jenquin's hardware store, two blocks away. At Jenquin's, the smiling clerk told me that he had just sold the last of their shore line. I walked back to the Pioneer and broke the bad news to Fred, and he doubled up with laughter. I should have known that the term "shore line" means property next to a body of water rather than a kind of rope. Later, Fred attempted to entrap me in several other of his pranks, but I now knew better. It was a learning experience.

The owner, Hal, was approximately fifty years old and casual in every regard, whether it be his clothing or his approach to the store. Although soft-spoken in manner, he also conveyed an attitude of indifference toward everything, with the exception of golf. He would often say, "Gotta see some people about some things," and drive off in his pickup truck. An hour or two later he would return, and no mention would ever be made of the people or of the things that he had looked into. It quickly became apparent, even to me, that Hal did not enjoy nor was he interested in the hardware business.

There was one more person who was a part of the usual routine at the store. Hal's father had founded the business fifty years earlier, and he would be in the store for several hours on most days. His daily uniform was a dark blue suit with a white shirt and a necktie, by far the best-dressed person in the store. He would stand in an out-of-the-way spot, as inconspicuous as possible, and watch what was going on with a look of disapproval on his face. Except for an occasional "Good morning," he remained silent throughout his stay. What I viewed as disapproval may have actually been dismay at the manner in which his son, and only child, was mismanaging the business he had worked so hard to develop. To say that he was stoic would have been an understatement.

When neither Hal nor his father were in the store, the employees would sometimes talk about them. We would dismissively refer to the old man as "Teddy," something we would never do were he present. One day I returned from an errand and, not seeing either Hal or his father, said, "I wonder where Teddy is today?" Fred looked at me with eyes bulging, and with a slight toss of his head directed my gaze to a dimly lit corner where the old man stood. Then Fred asked me, "Eddie who?" Fortunately, I caught on and replied "Eddie Brown. I haven't seen him in months." I did not know any Eddie Brown, but a crisis was averted. Later, Fred told me that if I had not come up with a name I would have been fired on the spot. I had grown comfortable, living the high life, on my pay of $2.80 each week, and I vowed that from now on I would make sure of my audience before speaking.

At first, my job was mainly that of a custodian, but my duties slowly expanded to include stocking shelves, waiting on customers, and assisting the repairman in delivering appliances. During the heating season, another of my duties was to carry the ashes from the furnace in the basement up to the alley behind the store, where they would be picked up for disposal. That was not particularly difficult, but it was the dirtiest part of my job.

There were three apartments above the store, and I would sweep and mop the hallway and stairs each Saturday. One of the tenants was a woman in her fifties with a son and daughter, both in their early twenties, and their radio would always be blaring loudly enough for me and anyone else on the floor to easily hear. One day, while I was sweeping the stairs, a well-dressed elderly man entered the building and began to walk up the stairs. Suddenly, when he was halfway up, the loud music abruptly stopped. He proceeded to their door and knocked on it many times before I, thinking I was being helpful, butted in and said, "There has to be someone in there." That motivated him to knock even louder, and as someone grudgingly opened the door, I returned to my sweeping. Later that day, the lady phoned Hal and complained about my intrusion into her affairs, and he then talked to me about it. He reminded me what my job was, and he told me not to pay any attention to the tenants. The unspoken message, which even I recognized, came through clearly: Mind your own business. Weeks later, I learned that the man who had knocked on the door was a bill collector. How the family could sense the arrival of the bill collector before his first knock on their door would remain a mystery.

It was a common practice for the tenants to put their wastebaskets outside their doors on Saturday morning, and I would empty and return them. The unusual family's trash would usually include a neatly typed sheet with what appeared to be the title of a story and below that a list of the characters. The top character would always be "Father Pat" and the actor would be Pat O'Brien, a popular American actor who happened to be from Wisconsin. Each Saturday, I anticipated some further evidence of an actual story or script, but that day never came. On almost every Saturday, however, there would be a new title and a list of characters, always headed by "Father Pat." That family remained an enigma to me for as long as I worked at the hardware store.

As I neared the magic age of sixteen, I began to look for a different job since sixteen was the age when one could legally be employed. On my final day at the Pioneer, Fred told me that the boy who had held my job before me had been paid seventy-five cents per hour. He had been a year older than me when hired and was the star of the golf team at the public high school. He had also been paid for the time he spent playing golf with Hal. I was unsure as to what I should do with this information so, true to form, I did nothing. The prospect of finally getting a "real" job blinded me to any injustice I may have experienced, and I continued to use the hardware store as my cut-through to downtown until it went out of business.

Although I had applied for work at several different businesses, J. C. Penney and Woolworth's, there was one job that I especially desired, and that was the one I got. Working at the Rialto Theatre as an usher and doorman (i.e., ticket-taker) seemed to me to be a perfect job. Wearing the bright blue blazer with gold buttons made me feel as though I were involved in something bigger than myself, and it was fun to be working with people, most of whom were my own age. The fact that the Rialto showed only second-run movies, some of which I had already seen, did not dampen my enthusiasm at all. Not only was I able to see movies free of charge; I was paid for the experience. My starting pay was forty-five cents per hour, and that was for a probationary period of the first three months. After that, my pay was bumped up to fifty cents per hour. The minimum wage at that time was seventy-five cents per hour but, as I recall, certain types of business were allowed to pay high school students a lower rate.

My workday at the Rialto started at 6:30 p.m. and ended at approximately 11:30 p.m. If it were the first day of a new showing, my first task would be to carry the film for the second feature up to the projection booth, located above the balcony. The projectionist would have already carried the feature film upstairs since that would be shown first.

Movies were distributed on large spools, and each spool had a running time of about fifteen minutes. The average movie consisted of six or seven spools, and it was delivered in two heavy steel octagonal-shaped cans. A full can weighed approximately fifty pounds. Carrying two cans up to the projection booth was one of the harder parts of that job.

Bill, the projectionist, was not a person who dressed for success. He dressed for comfort and often looked as though he just gotten out of bed. If his shirt and trousers matched or seemed to belong together, it was accidental. His hair shot out in all directions as if he had just gotten a jolt of electricity. He did not seem to consider personal grooming of great importance. Unlike the other employees who were expected to look professional, no such demands were made of him because the customers were unlikely to ever see him or to even be aware of him unless the equipment malfunctioned, and that rarely happened.

The most important position in a movie theatre at that time was that of the projectionist. If the theatre were an airplane, he would be the captain. On a train, he would be the engineer. The job required considerable training, as well as the ability to handle multiple details simultaneously within a confined area. The projection booth was small, approximately fifteen square feet, and there were two sizeable projectors and one rewinding machine crammed into it. Since a single spool held only fifteen minutes of film, the projectionist had to be alert for the cue, a tiny blinking dot in the upper right hand corner of the movie screen, the signal to push the floor pedal down to start the second projector. A competent operator could alternate between projectors so smoothly the audience would be unaware of it. After switching to the second spool, the operator would replace spool number one with the third spool and continue to alternate until all the spools, an entire movie, had been shown. Then it was on to the next movie. Most movie theatres, including the Rialto, showed double features, two movies for one ticket, so each night the main film would be shown twice and the secondary film once.

The job of the projectionist entailed other duties also. Once a spool was removed from the projector, it had to be rewound so that it would be ready for future use. Inside each projector was a lamphouse that housed two carbon arc rods, one positive and one negative. The electric charge from these rods provided blinding illumination, without which there would be no picture on the screen, and the rods had to be changed every twenty minutes. Occasionally, a film would break, and the operator would have to quickly splice the two loose ends together before the audience started registering their displeasure, and it did not take long for an audience to get upset. (When the screen went dark, there would be a groan. If it remained dark for a minute, there would be loud booing.) Besides those responsibilities, the projectionist also controlled the sound, curtain, and house lights and performed general maintenance on the equipment. The impressive array of switches, levers, and dials gave the booth the appearance of a control center, and that is exactly what it was. No matter what season of the year it was, the projection booth would be warm, if not hot, and Bill would enjoy the few free minutes he might have with his head out the small window, taking deep breaths of the fresh, often frosty, air while looking down onto Hall Avenue.

The job of an usher was approximately eighty percent pleasure and twenty percent actual work. Interacting with the ticket seller and the concessionaire, both of whom were teenage girls, was always fun. The fact that some of the girls attended public high school enhanced the experience since I viewed the public-school girls as more exotic than the classmates I saw every day.

The most arduous job an usher had to perform was "setting the canopy." Known to outsiders as a "marquee," to those of us "in the business" it was a canopy, and usually pronounced with a derisive inflection. The canopy was attached to the front of the theatre, ten feet above the sidewalk, and it extended out eight feet, the width of the sidewalk. Since there was a change of movies twice a week, the canopy had to be reset accordingly, and it had two sides. The task seems quite simple: 1) Get a ladder; 2) Remove the plastic letters advertising the previous feature film; 3) Replace them with the message that the manager had written down; 4) Repeat those steps on the other side of the canopy. However, just as is true of life in general, there could be complications.

The ten-foot wooden stepladder used for the job was stored on two short steel rods that had been driven into the outside back wall of the building, approximately four feet above the ground. For many years, the ladder had been bombarded by rain, snow, and ice, and it had not aged gracefully. It was completely waterlogged and so heavy that it had to be dragged rather than carried. The Rialto was situated between a bank and a popular restaurant, and the only way to move the ladder to the front was by dragging it around the outside of the restaurant. The total distance was nearly one hundred yards. By the time I would get the ladder upright and in proper position alongside the canopy, I would be breathing hard, but the work was just beginning.

I shared a kinship with the ladder since we were alike in our unsteadiness, although the ladder's case was more severe. It was in truly deplorable condition, having passed the rickety stage decades earlier, and every time I climbed up it was an adventure. The letters used in forming words on the marquee were made of heavy red plastic. Each letter was ten inches high and five inches wide and had several notches in its back. The notches would fit onto the small steel cables that were a part of the canopy. If there had snow or sleet recently, some of the letters would be frozen onto the cables and only pounding with the small of one's hand would dislodge them. Ushers were regularly reminded to be gentle with the letters as our supply of them was shrinking, and management did not plan to buy any more vowels, or consonants for that matter.

The ushers worked according to a schedule designed so that no one person had to set the canopy more often than the others; however, through no fault of management, it seemed to me that the weather was always bad when my turn came. I might have had a career as a rainmaker since I simply had to bring the ladder out and inclement weather was assured. Ushers were instructed to wait until after the intermission, between the first and second features, before attacking the canopy so it would be approximately 9:00 p.m. before the chore could begin. By that time, any hint of warmth would have been long gone.

After several months of winter, most residents will have grown comfortable with the predictable sameness of each day; however, on rare occasions a disruption may occur. Instead of the light snowfall that had been forecast for this night in late February, it was an ice storm that arrived as I began to set the canopy. A north wind coming over the river propelled tiny ice pellets that felt like needles when they struck exposed skin, and they would adhere to clothing as though it were Velcro. The longer you were exposed to such conditions, the heavier you felt, and I was beginning to feel like the puffed-up Michelin Man as I clung to the swaying ladder with my left hand and tried to manage the letters with my right. This weather was far from typical, but it contributed to what was to be a memorable night.

The message on the canopy was to be "DEHAVILLAND in HOLD BACK THE NIGHT." Olivia de Havilland was so well-known that no first name need be included, and that would be all right with anyone who had to set a canopy. Short names and brief titles were ideal. The fewer letters that had to be used, the better. (Alan Ladd in *Shane* was one of my favorites.) I had already completed one end of the canopy, dragged the ladder to the other end, and proceeded to affix the same message. There was a middle-aged lady sitting in a nearby car, probably waiting for someone in the theatre, and reading a book by the light provided by the many light bulbs on the canopy. After I had completed the canopy and dragged the ladder back to its rightful place behind the theatre, I was trudging to the front door to reenter the theater when the lady opened her car door and told me that I had misspelled a word. "de Havilland has two Ls, not one," she said. My "Thank you" probably lacked a ring of sincerity, but I retraced all of my steps and corrected my error. (I had spelled it correctly on the other side of the canopy.)

As I dragged the ladder past the restaurant for the fourth time that evening, I was preoccupied with feeling sorry for myself and did not notice that a small bolt, holding the bottom step of the ladder, was protruding slightly, until it snagged onto the shiny yellow slate front of the restaurant and dislodged a two-foot square section of the slate, which smashed into many small pieces on the sidewalk. The restaurant had just closed for the night. I had no idea what slate cost, but it had an expensive look to it, and I thought about nothing else in my classes the next day. After school, I went to the restaurant and talked to Mr. Schreiner, the owner. He might have been lying when he told me that he had been thinking of replacing that particular section, but I was not about to quibble with him. When he said that he would take care of it, I suddenly felt richer, not having to pay for the damage that I had caused. Many times our teachers told us that "Honesty is its own reward," but this was one instance in which it was accompanied by a monetary value.

At that time, Mary Lou had had a part-time job at J. C. Penney, and one day she came home from work and told me that the store was looking for another part-time employee. She said that if I went and talked to the manager the next day, I would probably be hired. The pay would be twenty-five cents more per hour than what I was currently earning, and I would get a sizeable discount on anything I bought. Also, there would be none of the late night hours that I was currently working. All the while she was telling me what a good job it would be, I was thinking, "You'd have to be crazy to expect me to quit my job in the glamorous and exciting movie business to go sell underwear and neckties, even if the pay was better." All I said, however, was "I think I'll stay at the Rialto for a while." She seemed surprised, but after making sure that I understood the wonderful opportunity I was rejecting, she dropped the matter. Being a movie lover herself, she did not question my decision, not even when I would occasionally complain about that "salt mine," the Rialto. Although she allowed me to make my own mistakes, she was always looking out for my best interests.

I graduated from high school in 1954 at age seventeen, and I worked that summer at a box factory in Menekaunee, a section of town that was originally a Native American fishing village. It was located near the mouth of the Menominee River, where the river empties into the bay. My pay was ninety cents per hour, and the plant operated five and a half days per week. One of the plant's major customers was the Kohler Plumbing Company, which was then in the midst of the nation's longest strike. I spent that summer helping make shipping crates for Kohler, which was located one hundred miles south. While the work itself was not physically taxing, the scream of the power saws and the sawdust-filled air combined to make each day a draining experience.

There was a large thermometer inside the plant. It was located above a message board that held the employees' timecards, next to the time clock that recorded when employees entered and departed the plant. During my first few weeks on the job, several of my coworkers had told me that if the thermometer reached one hundred degrees, the plant would shut down for the day. I filed that information away in my mind with the most unlikely events possible because northern Wisconsin is not known for high temperatures. Since the electric saw that I operated was a short distance from the thermometer, it was easy for me to constantly monitor it, and

I did. Other employee workstations were too far away to allow them to readily read the device unless they walked closer, and they did.

During one week in late July, the days were unusually warm, and a temperature of ninety degrees was recorded in the afternoon on both Monday and Tuesday, and on Wednesday it went as high as ninety-eight degrees. On Thursday, when the high temperature was eighty-eight degrees, the disappointment was palpable, but on Friday at 2:45, miraculously, the temperature reached one hundred degrees. The factory steam whistle sounded, and a cheer went up from the employees who turned off their saws and lined up by the time clock with speed unlike any demonstrated that summer. I had never seen this group as upbeat and talkative as they were as they waited to punch out. Most of them were singing the praises of the owner, "a good man," and his enlightened policy. A few others were talking about enjoying the unexpected break at the Sailor's Inn, the nearest tavern. The euphoria of the group led me to believe that we would be paid for the hours not worked. I was wrong.

During the decade of the 1950s, the nation heaved a sigh of relief, happy that the war had ended and pleased with the idea that life was slowly returning to normal. It was not a time of rapid change, but one noteworthy development was the effective polio vaccine created by Dr. Jonas Salk. Parents, without any hesitation, rushed to get their children vaccinated, and eventually the dreaded disease was eliminated. This was also the decade in which the first McDonald's restaurant opened in the US, although it would be decades before one appeared in Marinette.

The wheels of change may revolve more slowly in smaller towns, and that is thought to be one of the positive aspects of living away from the hustle of a metropolitan area. Change is inevitable, however, and eventually it affected the town as well as my family. After their building was destroyed by a fire, the Farmers and Merchants Bank bought our house, demolished it, and built a modern bank at that location. Both Pat and Mary Lou were married and away from home by that time, and we moved to a smaller house on the same block. Char loved becoming a step-grandmother, and she was wonderful in that role. My father stubbornly resisted change as much as possible, and he remained the kindhearted, honest, and hardworking individual that he had always been. A salesman from the Hobart welding supplies company told him that his Hobart arc welder was the oldest one still in use in the nation. Something else that never changed were the frigid temperatures in the blacksmith shop every winter.

See You Later, Alligator

That fall I enrolled at Saint Norbert College in DePere, Wisconsin, sixty miles from home. After the first semester I was on probation due to poor grades, and after the second semester wason the dean's list with good grades. Never for the next three years would my name grace either of those lists again. My major was business administration, and I joined the Collegiate Players and enjoyed acting in plays, just as in high school. Writing for the college newspaper also provided pleasure, satisfaction, and challenges.

As graduation approached, I became increasingly concerned about my future since I had no idea what I wanted to do with my life. One of my professors, Lee Dudek, who taught me in a class, and directed me in a play, was supportive and assured me that my feelings were not uncommon. He was an interesting person, subdued in the classroom, but volatile and self-assured as a director. His face would redden like an apple at harvest time as he voiced his displeasure or "suggested" a better way to accomplish something. Rehearsals could be tense and result in frayed nerves, however, most students recognized that following his instruction not only led to improved performance, but also to shorter rehearsals. Although Dudek was not a person prone to understatement, understated he was the spring day that he predicted that it might take "a while" for me to find the right job, but that it would happen eventually.

Following graduation from St. Norbert I enrolled in law school at the University of Wisconsin, as my father had been urging me to do. He envisioned me practicing law in Marinette, but that was not to be. After two semesters of studying contracts, torts, and property law, I could not imagine a lifetime immersed in such matters. I next moved to Milwaukee to continue my search for the "right" job, went to work for an insurance company, and awaited an "invitation" from the government.

My draft notice arrived a few months after I had dropped out of law school, and I was soon immersed in basic training at Fort Leonard Wood in Missouri. Basic training lasted eight weeks, six days per week, and ten to twelve hours per day. Training was rigorous, and spare time non-existent. No two days were alike, but there were several experiences that made a lasting impression. One involved a simulated nighttime battle in which the trainees had to crawl on their stomachs, using their elbows and knees for locomotion, M1 rifle cradled in the crook of their arms, for approximately twenty-five yards. Staying low was essential as you crawled under low-hanging barbwire fences while shells from fifty caliber machine guns were whizzing overhead. Every fourth or fifth shell was a tracer designed to show the path of the shells. The tracers were also intended to remind the troops to keep heads and butts down, not that any reminder was necessary. Controlled explosions, sending dirt into the air, were occurring all around you, providing additional realism. The darkness, the noise, the gun smoke, and the dirt-laden air combined to create complete chaos. It was enough to make a person think that, perhaps, they should have stayed in college.

The tear gas exercise provided another experience that made me question my current career path, whatever it was. After an hour of instruction on proper gas mask usage, the trainees, gas masks on, lined up next to a small igloo-shaped building made of corrugated steel. Brought inside in groups of five or six, when approached by an instructor, who himself was well protected by a perfectly fitted gas mask, each trainee had to stand at attention, remove their gas mask, and slowly and clearly state their name and eight digit service number. Then they were to put their mask back on and slowly exit the building, removing their masks, only after sitting down on a nearby wooden bleacher. It seemed a simple and straight forward means of imparting the importance of gas masks for the modern soldier, and I was brimming with confidence as I entered the building. When the instructor approached me for the required information, standing at attention I removed my mask with such a flourish that it flew out of my hand, and I had to crawl on my hands and knees to retrieve it. The dim lighting complicated my search as did the air, heavily laden with tear gas.

JAMES LAHIFF

The laughter of the instructor was not helpful either. By the time I stood up and wheezed out my name and number, however, the instructor's face had lost any trace of the laugh I had heard, and once again bore the standard, military-issue stoic gaze that was universal among the training cadre. Whenever I had an unpleasant experience in basic training, and there weren't that many, I consoled myself with the knowledge that it would end soon, and I would be enjoying life in a more appealing locale.

Following basic training I was sent to Fort Gordon, Georgia for eight weeks of advanced training in the Signal Corps. After that training I would be assigned to what would be "home" for the next eighteen months. Early in the seventh week of training, travel orders began trickling in. The government paid six cents per mile travel pay, and some of my classmates learned of their travel pay before discovering their destination. Germany and Italy wereconsidered most desirable, and troops going there were receiving travel pay of approximately two hundred dollars. When I learned that my travel pay would be thirty cents, I assumed that a mistake had been made, but was informed that "They never make mistakes." My hopes for an assignment to Europe were dashed. While classmates were departing for Germany, Italy, California, New Jersey, and other exotic locations, I packed my duffel bag, boarded the local bus, and rode five miles to the other side of Fort Gordon, and to the 40th Signal Battalion, my new home.

For the next eighteen months I worked as a clerk in the 40th's headquarters where I handled a wide variety of paperwork. The battalion consisted of approximately eight hundred troops, and the days flew by. The man that I reported to was Sergeant Major Homer L. Dukes Jr. The rank of sergeant major is the highest rank attainable among non-commissioned officers, and only a miniscule number ever reach it. Born in rural North Carolina, he was plain-spoken, completely lacking in glibness or slickness, and he set high standards for himself and for the enlisted men working at headquarters. He led by example, and was the most effective leader I have ever been around. He kept us aware of pertinent rules and regulations but, if the situation called for it, he could be pragmatic.

When Headquarters began receiving three or four phone calls each week that were intended for a taxicab service, it was discovered that the two telephone numbers were nearly identical. When Dukes contacted the telephone company, requesting that the phone number of the taxi service be changed, he was told that such a change would not be possible for at least one year. Frustrated by that information he instructed his staff to tell any caller seeking a taxi, "We'll be right over," and added, "We'll see what happens." In less that one month the taxi service had a new phone number.

My twenty-five month sojourn in the army provided me with ample leisure time to accomplish many things. Learning a foreign language, acquiring new hobbies, and taking college correspondence courses were some of the options that were readily available. It would have been a fine time for me to contemplate my future, to establish possible career goals, and to prioritize those goals. Unfortunately, I did none of those things, but instead spent hours with friends, bemoaning our plight of being "stuck" in the Army while the world passed us by. These lamentation sessions were usually held off-base in downtown Augusta and were accompanied by adult beverages. Since we were paid on the first of the month, we went to town more often early in the month. Trips became less frequent (and drier) towards the end o the month as our funds dwindled. With the start of a new month, the cycle would repeat itself.

A month after receiving an honorable discharge I moved to Milwaukee, found an apartment with a friend from college, and began my job search, a search that was hampered by my continuing inability to decide what to do with my life. A major reason for going to work at the Milwaukee Association of Commerce Credit Bureau was because it was possible to have a flexible schedule, and my plan was to take some college courses while working full time. Much of my job was devoted to investigating the credit and employment history of individuals who had applied for credit or for employment at certain companies. I gathered the necessary information by talking to sources on the telephone. The job was enjoyable as were my co-workers.

During the four years that I worked there, I applied for two other jobs: one at an advertising agency and the other at the Milwaukee Sentinel, the city's morning newspaper. When interviewed at the ad agency, the more I learned about the position, the better suited I considered myself for it. Unfortunately, the interviewer did not share that sentiment. At the Sentinel I was interviewed by one of the editors, who said that he would hire me as a reporter if I first got a job at a small town newspaper and worked there for six months. I was enjoying the fast pace and bright lights of the big city too much to even consider such a drastic move, so my search continued for the "right" job.

It happened when I was enrolled in a Psychology of Communication course taught by Professor Frank Dance at UWM, the University of Wisconsin Milwaukee. The subject matter was interesting, but it was Dance's approach to teaching that especially intrigued me. Not only was he intelligent and enthusiastic, he enjoyed teaching so much that his enjoyment was contagious and infected the students. He created a unique learning environment, distinctly different from anything I had ever experienced. To call it an "epiphany" might be an overstatement, however, it was an "Ah-Ha" moment and I, at long last, realized what my path would be, and I had the GI Bill to help me reach my goal.

Thinking back to my early years in Marinette, there are certain positives and negatives that come to mind. A major downside was the high expectations that life in Marinette created in the minds of residents, expectations that often went unmet if they moved to a different community. While there was little ethnic diversity, there was much diversity of thought and opinion. Most adults seemed to feel that they knew what the government should or should not be doing. I enjoyed being able to witness many discussions, and a few arguments, on such matters at the blacksmith shop which, like the town itself, was a special place.

One of my many happy memories of my childhood involves sledding on an unimposing hill next to the library. Although the hill was steep, it was not high enough to attract kids from other neighborhoods, most of whom would sled at City Park, which had more challenging hills, but it was conveniently close to home for us. Starting in the middle of November, after the first snowfall, we would often go there. The hill flattened out on to a small field that bordered the river. On rare occasions, a sled would build up enough speed to cross the field and slide on to the solid ice of the river. Any sledder who accomplished that feat would be proclaimed the champion for that day. Most days there would be no champion, but it was fun to try.

Since the hill was adjacent to the interstate bridge, there would be a steady flow of heavy traffic passing by. Flatbed trailer trucks laden with Christmas trees were a common sight, and we would snicker about those "poor suckers" in Milwaukee, Chicago, and towns south who had no choice but to buy dried-out trees that had been cut six weeks before Christmas. We all agreed that we were lucky to live where our Christmas trees were always freshly cut, and we were indeed lucky to live in that place at that time.

Employment History

Marinette Eagle-Star
Pioneer Hardware
Fox/Rialto Theatres
McClellan's, Inc.
A&P
M&M Box Company
Scott Paper Company
US Postal Service
H C Prange, Inc.
Shorty & Lammy's Brauthaus (Madison)
New York Life Insurance (Milwaukee)
US Army (40th Signal Battalion)
Milwaukee Association of Commerce Credit Bureau
Pennsylvania State University
University of Georgia

A. J. LAHIFF
BLACKSMITH - WELDER
ESTABLISHED 1881
ACETYLENE AND ELECTRIC WELDING
SHOP AT 613 WELLS STREET

Marinette, Wis., _____ 19___

VOTE FOR
ALVIN (AL) J.
LAHIFF
REPUBLICAN CANDIDATE FOR
SHERIFF
ABLE - HONEST
ENERGETIC

Authorized and paid for by Alvin J. Lahiff, whose P. O address is Marinette, Wis. FABRY PRTG.

CPSIA information can be obtained
at www.ICGtesting.com
Printed in the USA
BVHW071649090622
639361BV00001B/78